WORLD WAR II
THE DEFEAT OF THE NAZIS:
THE ALLIED VICTORY IN EUROPE

WORLD WAR II

THE DEFEAT OF THE NAZIS: THE ALLIED VICTORY IN EUROPE

MASON CREST

Mason Crest
450 Parkway Drive, Suite D
Broomall, PA 19008
www.masoncrest.com

© 2018 by Mason Crest, an imprint of National Highlights, Inc.

Cataloging-in-Publication Data on file with the Library of Congress.

Printed and bound in the United States of America.

First printing
9 8 7 6 5 4 3 2 1

ISBN: 978-1-4222-3897-4
Series ISBN: 978-1-4222-3893-6
ebook ISBN: 978-1-4222-7907-6
ebook series ISBN: 978-1-4222-7903-8

Produced by Regency House Publishing Limited
The Manor House
High Street
Buntingford
Hertfordshire
SG9 9AB
United Kingdom

www.regencyhousepublishing.com

Text copyright © 2018 Regency House Publishing Limited/Christopher Chant.

PAGE 2: Men of one of the two German parachute divisions committed to the Ardennes operations.

PAGE 3: Soviet infantry of an elite guards unit attack in the summer of 1943.

RIGHT: A German painting of the Messerschmitt Bf 110 heavy fighter, shown in action in its most important night-fighter role.

PAGE 6: Men of the U.S. 82nd Airborne Division prepare for their part in the Arnhem operation, namely the capture of the bridge over the Maas river at Grave.

CONTENTS

KEY ICONS TO LOOK FOR:

 Words to Understand: These words with their easy-to-understand definitions will increase the reader's understanding of the text, while building vocabulary skills.

 Sidebars: This boxed material within the main text allows readers to build knowledge, gain insights, explore possibilities, and broaden their perspectives by weaving together additional information to provide realistic and holistic perspectives.

 Educational Videos: Readers can view videos by scanning our QR codes, providing them with additional content to supplement the text. Examples include news coverage, moments in history, speeches, iconic sports moments, and much more!

 Text-Dependent Questions: These questions send the reader back to the text for more careful attention to the evidence presented here.

 Research Projects: Readers are pointed toward areas of further inquiry connected to each chapter. Suggestions are provided for projects that encourage deeper research and analysis.

 Series Glossary of Key Terms: This back-of-the-book glossary contains terminology used throughout the series. Words found here increase the reader's ability to read and comprehend high-level books and articles in this field.

OPPOSITE: Operation Overlord: American troops having loaded their equipment in a landing craft tank await the signal to leave for the continent.

National World War II Memorial

The National World War II Memorial in Washington, D.C., is dedicated to the 16 million people who served in the American armed forces during World War II. The memorial also honors the 400,000 who gave the ultimate sacrifice for their country. Those who supported the war effort at home are honored too. The memorial symbolizes World War II as the defining event of the 20th century.

The memorial is situated on a 7.4-acre (3-hectare) site. It was created by designer and architect Friedrich St. Florian who won a national open competition for its design. The construction of memorial took place between 2001 and 2004 and then opened to the public on April 29, 2004; its official dedication took place a month later, on May 29. It was commission by President Clinton in 1993 who authorized the American Battle Monuments Commission (ABMC) to establish a World War II memorial in the Washington, D.C. area.

The memorial is an elliptical shaped plaza built around a splendid fountain and pool, with water jets in its center. Built in a semi-classical style, there are 56 granite columns forming a semi-circle around the perimeter. Each one is designed to symbolize the unity of the states, federal territories, and District of Columbia. The entry walkway is flanked by ornate balustrades decorated with 24 bronze bas-reliefs.

At the mid point of the plaza there are two pavilions decorated with bronzes, featuring Baldachins, American Eagles, and World War II Victory Medals. The pavilions represent the Atlantic and Pacific theaters.

At the western end of the memorial is a curved Freedom Wall bearing a field of 4,048 golden stars, each of which stands for 100 American military deaths in the war. Before it lies a granite curb inscribed "Here we mark the price of freedom."

Throughout the memorial are inscribed quotations from eminent military and political figures, including Gen. (later Pres.) Dwight D. Eisenhower, U.S. Presidents Franklin D. Roosevelt and Harry S. Truman, Col. Oveta Culp Hobby, Adm. Chester W. Nimitz, Gen. George C. Marshall, and Gen. Douglas MacArthur.

The National World War II Memorial is located at the east end of the Reflecting Pool on the Mall, opposite the Lincoln Memorial and west of the Washington Monument. The memorial is maintained by the U.S. National Park Service, and receives almost 5 million visitors each year. It is open 24 hours a day and is free to all visitors.

WORLD WAR II
Chapter One
THE BATTLE OF KURSK

The destruction of the 6th Army in Stalingrad proved that the Germans were not invincible and that the Soviets had an effective army, while the Battle of Kursk five months later showed that Germany could not hope to win the war with the USSR. This great armored clash was the last time that Germany was able to take the initiative on the Eastern Front. Fighting on ground of their own choosing, and at a time they considered best for their tactics, the German armies were first halted and then thrown back by the size and skill of the constantly improving Soviet forces.

With the spring thaw in March 1943, operations on the Eastern Front came to a temporary halt, and the Germans at last had the time to plan their next move, although the planning staffs in Germany were severely taxed as to what this move might be. The Oberkommando der Wehrmacht (OKW, or armed forces high command), which ran the German war effort in every theater but the USSR, was of the opinion that the German armies

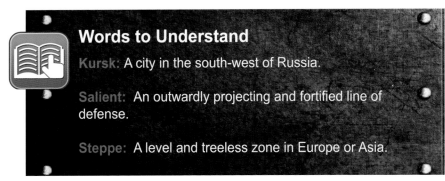

Words to Understand

Kursk: A city in the south-west of Russia.

Salient: An outwardly projecting and fortified line of defense.

Steppe: A level and treeless zone in Europe or Asia.

there should go over to the strategic defensive, and so free forces for the western theaters, in which the great Allied invasion was expected shortly. The Oberkommando des Heeres (OKH, or army high command), which ran the war against the USSR under Hitler's overall supervision, agreed with OKW to a certain extent, but thought it essential that there be a limited German offensive in the USSR during the summer to spoil any Soviet intentions for offensive action.

Hitler agreed with the OKH, principally because he felt that a striking victory was needed to bolster the flagging spirits of his European allies.

Once they had decided that a limited offensive was needed, the OKH planners decided that the best place to strike such a blow was the great salient jutting into the German lines west of Kursk. The trouble was that this was an obvious choice for such an offensive, so speed of planning and execution was vital if tactical surprise was to be achieved. The German plan was in essence simple, and was based on the familiar pincer theory. Field-Marshal Walther Model's 9th Army of Army Group Center, commanded by Field-Marshal Günther von Kluge, was to advance on Kursk from the northern half of the salient, while Colonel-General Hermann Hoth's 4th Panzerarmee and General Wilhelm Kempf's Armeeabteilung Kempf, both supplied by Field-Marshal Erich von Manstein's Army Group South, were to advance on Kursk from the south. The Central and Voronezh Fronts would be trapped in the salient and then destroyed, after which German forces would be freed for service in the west.

The OKH wished the offensive, codenamed Zitadelle (citadel), to take place as early in April as possible after the spring mud had dried out enough to

allow armored vehicles to function. But no sooner had the basic plan been formulated than reasons for delay began to pour in: troops could not be moved up in time, and Model decided that his forces were not sufficient for the task in hand. The April date passed, as did one in May, and at this stage several senior commanders began to have second thoughts about the whole operation: of these the two most important were General Alfred Jodl, chief of the OKW operations staff, and Colonel-General Heinz Guderian, recently recalled to service as inspector-general of armored forces following his dismissal after the battle for Moscow Both these men considered the offensive to be very dangerous in concept and that it should be abandoned. Guderian also felt that the new Panther battle tanks and Elefant tank-destroyers would be wasted, the divisions which were to use them having not yet been able to train properly. Hitler himself began to have doubts, as did von Manstein, but Field-Marshal Wilhelm Keitel, head of the OKW, and Colonel-General Kurt Zeitzler, the OKH chief of staff, managed to overcome Hitler's misgivings. The offensive was finally scheduled for July, by which time ample supplies of ammunition, troops, and new tanks would be available, it was believed.

OPPOSITE: Protected by the thick armor of a tank from German air attack, Soviet officers plan their next move on the Eastern Front in 1943. By this time the Soviet forces were very nearly the equal of the German armies in essential weapons and fighting skills.

ABOVE: German armor on the move near Kharkov in the summer of 1943. Lying in a German salient, and biting into the underside of the Soviet salient around Kursk, this was at the heart of the fighting that followed Germany's strategic defeat in the Battle of Kursk in July 1943.

RIGHT: Soviet infantry move into the ruined outskirts of Belgorod, to the north of Kharkov, as the Soviets sweep over to the counteroffensive after their triumph in the Battle of Kursk.

Utmost secrecy was to be observed as the preparations for the attack were made.

Despite the German precautions in the matter of secrecy, the Soviets were kept fully informed of all that was happening by their in-country intelligence system and Swiss-based "Lucy" ring, whose main asset was probably a person working in the high-level communications or coding department in Berlin. By such means, the Soviet Stavka (high command) was able to keep a close watch on the progress of German preparations and make its own plans accordingly. Just about the only thing the Soviets did not know was the time appointed for the actual attack, but

they were to be told of this too by a deserter before the offensive began. Although they did not know it, the German armies were to attack without any element of strategic surprise, and in only a few places did the first attacking formations achieve any measure of tactical surprise.

With the exception of the immediate German start lines, the Kursk salient is excellent terrain for armored warfare, with low rolling hills of firm sandy soil and relatively few towns, the whole dotted with sunflower fields and orchards. Accordingly, the Germans massed most of their mobile forces to the north and south of the salient. Model's

9th Army totaled some six Panzer, one Panzergrenadier and 14 infantry divisions, although only eight of the infantry divisions were to be used in Zitadelle. Supported by some 730 aircraft of Luftflotte 6's 1st Fliegerdivision, the 9th Army was able to field about 900 tanks, although most of these were obsolescent PzKpfw II, PzKpfw III, and early PzKpfw IV types. In the south, von Manstein had more numerous and better-equipped forces: nine Panzer, two Panzergrenadier and 11 infantry divisions, although only seven of the infantry divisions were to be used in the planned offensive. More significantly, von Manstein's forces had some 1,000 tanks and 150 assault guns, these armored fighting vehicles including about 200 of the new PzKpfw V Panther battle tanks and 94 of the new and even more powerful PzKpfw Tiger I heavy tanks. Air support was provided by the 1,100 aircraft of Luftflotte 4's VIII Fliegerkorps. Artillery support comprised some 6,000 guns and mortars in the north, and 4,000 weapons in the south.

This was a formidable offensive force but one with distinct limitations. The most important of these were the fact that many formations had only recently been reorganized after the debacle at Stalingrad and Germany's subsequent defeat in the south. They had not achieved their true potential as

fighting units as yet, trained reserves and replacements were in short supply, and although Hitler and the staff generals had high expectations of the new armored vehicles, Guderian and the front-line commanders were all too aware that these had been rushed into premature action, and were still very prone to teething troubles. The Panther, Tiger, and Elefant were all somewhat unreliable mechanically, the Elefant suffering from the distinct tactical

disadvantage of having no defensive machine gun with which to ward off close-range infantry attack.

Even so, the Soviets were leaving nothing to chance, and were massing truly enormous forces in the Kursk salient for the forthcoming battle. The overall plan was devised by Georgi Zhukov, promoted to Marshal of the Soviet Union in January 1943. Zhukov was not content with merely stopping the Germans' attempt to eliminate the Kursk salient. Once the German forces were firmly embedded in the Soviet defenses of the salient proper, massive offensives were to be launched into the German counter-salients north and south of Kursk in the regions of Orel and Kharkov. The whole Soviet front was then to grind forward remorselessly. In the Kursk salient proper, the Soviets had had four months in which to prepare their defenses, based on a series of very strong field fortifications. The first line consisted of five lines of trenches some 3 miles (5km) deep, reinforced with numerous antitank strongpoints. In this area, antitank and antipersonnel mines were laid at a density of 2,400 and 2,700 mines per mile of front. Some 7 miles (11km) behind the first line lay a similar second line, with a strong third line 20 miles (32km) behind the second. Behind

this third line were the front reserves, dug into formidable defenses of their own. Finally there were the theater reserves, the Reserve or Steppe Front, commanded by the redoubtable Colonel-General I.S. Konev, holding the neck of the salient. Here could be formed a final line of defense should the Germans break through that far; at the same time, the salient could not be cut off and there was the capability of reinforcing either of the two first-line fronts.

In the salient were General K.K. Rokossovsky's Central Front, facing Model, and General N.F. Vatutin's Voronezh Front, facing von Manstein. It was Rokossovsky who had astutely suggested the location of the **Steppe** Front at the neck of the salient. Even allowing for differences in designation (a Soviet army being equivalent to a strengthened western corps, and a Soviet corps to a reinforced western division), it is clear that the three fronts were very strong. The Central Front had one tank and five infantry armies, as well as two tank corps; the Voronezh Front had one tank and five infantry armies, together with one infantry and two tank corps; and the Steppe Front had one tank and four infantry armies, with the support of a further one tank, one mechanized and three cavalry corps. The numbers of Soviet troops were therefore considerable,

Otto Moritz Walther Model (1891–1945)

Model was a German field marshal during World War II. He is noted for his defensive battles in the latter half of the war, mostly on the Eastern Front but also in the west. He has been called the Third Reich's best defensive tactical commander.
At Kursk the northern half of the planned German pincer operation was the responsibility of Colonel-General Walther Model, seen here, whose 9th Army failed to make any but the most limited inroads into the Soviet defenses.

OPPOSITE ABOVE: In the Battle of Kursk the Germans made use, prematurely, of a new generation of fighting vehicles, whose developmental problems had not been wholly overcome. This is a PzKpfw VI Tiger I heavy tank of the 2nd SS Panzer Division Das Reich.

OPPOSITE BELOW: Tanks of the 3rd SS Panzergrenadier Division Totenkopf, on the move in the first stages of the Battle of Kursk during July 1943. The German army was everywhere impeded by the density of the Soviet minefields, antitank ditches and concentrated artillery fire, before having to fight it out with massed Soviet armor.

RIGHT: Guderian being transported to the Eastern Front, 1943.

and so too were the matériel resources available to them: 13,000 guns, 6,000 antitank guns, and 1,000 rocket-launchers for the two forward fronts, some 2,500 aircraft deployed by the 2nd and 16th Air Armies, and at least 3,600 armored fighting vehicles, although some Soviet sources put the figure as high as 5,000. The Battle of Kursk was therefore to see the deployment of at least 5,600 armored fighting vehicles – perhaps even 7,000 such machines.

The Soviets knew what the Germans were planning. The Germans, however, had no comparable source within the Soviet high command, and their reconnaissance aircraft had failed to reveal the extent and thoroughness of the Soviet preparations. Having carried all before them in the air for the first two years of the Soviet war, the warplanes of the Luftwaffe had at last been matched by Soviet aircraft. Superior Soviet numbers and an increasing level of skill were to prevail in the long run. The Soviets demonstrated at Kursk that heavy tactical air support of ground forces, with masses of aircraft such as the excellent Ilyushin Il-2 Shturmovik, would prove decisive.

All was finally ready on July 5, after a delay occasioned by Soviet artillery bombardment of the German forming-up areas. There was an intense two-hour bombardment of the Soviet positions,

and then the 9th Army attacked. The bombardment failed to crush the Soviet defenses, and the one infantry and three Panzer corps immediately encountered stiff resistance. By July 11 Model had fed into the battle all the forces available to him, but the maximum penetration along the 30-mile (50-km) offensive front was a mere 15 miles (25km in the region of Ponyri and Olkhovatka. Near these two villages the Soviet 2nd Tank Army put up a magnificent defense, and furious armored battles raged at very close quarters. Although the latest German tanks had good armor and armament, making them formidable opponents at long range, the Soviets used the superior mobility and speed of their tanks to keep at close range, where their inferior armament was just as good as the Germans' long-barreled 2.95- and 3.465-inch (75- and 88-mm) guns. In one small area were engaged some 2,000 tanks and self-propelled guns, the losses on both sides being extremely heavy. The 9th Army was now exhausted, the German advance slowed and finally stopped just short of the ridge, after which it was downhill all the way to Kursk. Rokossovsky's forces had broken the northern arm of the pincer intended to eliminate the Kursk salient, causing Model to lose 25,000 dead, more than 200 of his tanks, and more than 200 of Luftflotte 6's aircraft.

In the south, von Manstein attacked earlier, and at first enjoyed better results, largely as a result of his tactics. With a high infantry/armor ratio, Model had decided to use conventional tactics, with infantry, engineers, and artillery opening the way for the tanks to move up. Von Manstein, on the other hand, did not have the infantry for such tactics, and decided instead to use his armor to open the way for the supporting forces. The tactic evolved to meet von Manstein's need was the Panzerkeil (armor wedge), with a Panther or Tiger at the head of the wedge, and PzKpfw III and PzKpfw IV tanks fanning out behind it along the sides of the wedge. During the battle, von Manstein realized this formation was wrong, since the Soviet tanks were closing in to a range where the new tanks' superior guns could not be used to full advantage. He changed the composition of the wedge so that the older tanks were leading to flush the Soviet tanks and antitank guns, while the Panther or Tiger followed behind to engage the flushed target at long range.

The 4th Panzerarmee, which was to strike for Kursk by way of Oboyan, made good progress through the Soviet 6th Guards Army, but then ran into the 1st Tank Army and was slowed. At the same time, Armeeabteilung Kempf struck north-east from just south of Belgorod to protect the 4th Panzerarmee's right flank from Soviet reinforcements coming in from the east. By July 6 both the 4th Panzerarmee and Armeeabteilung Kempf had driven deep into the Soviet defenses, but the Soviet reserves were beginning to arrive in considerable numbers, the most important of these being the 5th Guards Tank Army, an elite and powerful armored force. Determined resistance was gradually overcome, and by 11 July, Hoth's left wing, with the XLVIII Panzer Corps as its main striking element, had pushed forward some 15 miles (25km) against the 40th, 6th Guards, and 1st Tank Armies. On Hoth's right wing, the II SS Panzer Corps, under the command of General Paul Hausser, was making even better progress, and had pushed forward as far as Prokhorovka after an advance of 30 miles (50km). The Armeeabteilung Kempf was also moving

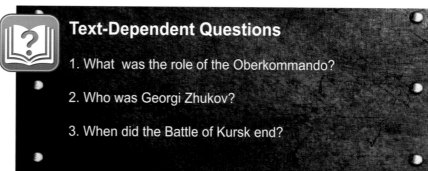

Text-Dependent Questions

1. What was the role of the Oberkommando?

2. Who was Georgi Zhukov?

3. When did the Battle of Kursk end?

Research Projects

Summarize the main reasons why the Battle of Kursk was unsuccessful for the Germans.

forward well and had reached Rzhavets on the upper Donets, with a line of Soviet forces keeping it separated from the II SS Panzer Corps. On July 12 the head of the 5th Guards Tank Army reached Prokhorovka, engaging the tanks of the SS Panzer corps, and the largest tank battle in history was about to start.

Hausser's tanks and their crews were by now in fairly poor shape, but the Soviets were able to stop their advance on only the first engagement. With more Soviet tanks on the way, Hausser's position was just becoming precarious when the III Panzer Corps, the spearhead of the Armeeabteilung Kempf, arrived from the upper Donets to take the 5th Guards Tank Army in flank. The battle was confused and desperate, but late on July 13 the Germans seemed to be gaining the upper hand. On this day, however, von Manstein and von Kluge

OPPOSITE: German Panzer IV and Sdkfz 251 halftrack.

ABOVE: Soviet machine gun crew during the Battle of Kursk.

had been summoned to a meeting with Hitler, who told them that Zitadelle was to be called off, for the Allies had landed in Sicily three days before and more troops were needed in the west. A day earlier, moreover, the Central, West and Bryansk Fronts had launched a great offensive against von Kluge's Army Group Center. Model's small gains were wiped out almost immediately, and by August 18 the German salient around Orel had been eliminated, so von Kluge was only too pleased to hear of the cancellation of Zitadelle. But von Manstein was not happy with the decision. Although he had been against the operation from the start, he now felt he was in a position to destroy a major portion of the Soviet armored strength in the battle around Prokhorovka. Hitler reluctantly agreed, and von Manstein urged Hausser to complete the destruction of the 5th Guards Tank Army as swiftly as possible. Just as victory was in sight, however, on July 17 Hitler ordered the attack to be broken off, and the SS Panzer corps sent to Italy. The Battle of Kursk was over: it had failed in its major objective, and had in the end also failed in the ad hoc objective of destroying the Soviet armor, just as the distinct possibility of victory had come into sight.

On August 3 the Voronezh, Steppe, and South-West Fronts went over to the general offensive, and by August 23 the Kharkov salient had fallen once again to the Soviets. A general offensive had now started right along the Soviet line from west of Moscow south to the Black Sea, and in a series of coordinated attacks, which ended only on December 23, the Soviets drove Army Groups Center, South and A to the line of the Dniepr river. The 17th Army was cut off in Crimea, and the Soviets also secured huge bridgeheads across the Dniepr from north of Gomel to south of Kiev (these fell on November 6) and between Kremenchug and Zaporozhye.

The most significant event of the year had been the German failure to eliminate the Kursk salient. This was the last time the Germans were to hold the initiative on the Eastern Front, and from this time on all they could do was to attempt to maintain their hold. Hitler steadfastly refused to sanction retreat, but the weight and size of the Soviet forces gradually drove the Germans back, despite the latter's great skill and determination in defensive fighting. Stalingrad had signaled the high point of the German advance, but Kursk signaled the beginning of the decline.

WORLD WAR II
Chapter Two
THE ALLIED INVASION OF ITALY

As the last battles were being fought in Tunisia, the Allied staffs were already planning the invasion of Italy. Although a heavy toll had been taken of them on land and in the air, the Axis forces were still able to offer strong resistance and it was believed, especially by General Sir Bernard Montgomery, that the Italians would fight hard in defense of their own soil. Allied air forces were waging a war of attrition against the Luftwaffe and Regia Aeronautica, but Axis warplanes could still be a menace to the ships of an amphibious operation, so it was necessary to advance step-by-step within range of land-based fighter cover. The intention was to capture Sicily, with its airfields, and then, as the opportunity arose, cross over to the toe and heel of the mainland. However, the next main thrust would again be made by sea to a point south of Naples, but still within range of effective air cover.

The expedition was to be a combined U.S. and British undertaking supervised by a supreme commander based in Africa (at first the U.S. General Dwight D. Eisenhower, and then the British General Sir Maitland Wilson). General Sir Harold Alexander's 15th Army Group was to command the two field armies, Lieutenant-General George S. Patton's U.S. 7th, and Montgomery's British 8th Armies. In terms of numbers, the assault on Sicily was to be the biggest amphibious operation so far attempted. On the right, the 8th Army, preceded by a brigade of gliderborne troops, was to land on the east coast with four divisions, turn right and advance north, making for the Strait of Messina and so cut off all the Axis troops on the island. On the left, the 7th Army was to land three divisions, with an armored division close behind, on a 50-mile (80- km) front on the south coast. It was to be preceded by four battalions of parachute troops, whose task was to seize airfields and other vital points inland. Patton's role was to protect the flank and rear of the 8th Army from interference by the six Axis divisions in the island, two of them Panzer or Panzergrenadier formations of the highest quality.

This was a perfectly good plan, but it was plain to the Americans that Alexander had selected the British 8th Army for the decisive role, and resented the fact. Some U.S. divisions had in fact not performed well in their first actions in Tunisia, but they were now blooded and anxious to show their form. No one, however, resented the slur more than Patton, a brilliant, highly temperamental, and intensely patriotic officer who, to make matters worse, strongly disliked the able, but arrogant and tactless General Montgomery.

From 1943, the tremendous power of the Allies, especially in the air, made the chances of failure remote, but they were still inexperienced. Amphibious landings are always hazardous and the opening phase of this operation was almost a disaster. On the day that Operation Husky was launched on July 10, Montgomery's troops disembarked efficiently, consolidated, and moved off to capture their first objective, the naval base of Syracuse. But the entire airborne operation was a fiasco. The U.S. Troop Carrier Command was really a logistic force: its pilots were unaccustomed to flying in the combat zone and incapable of the pinpoint navigation required for airborne operations at night. Confused by bad weather and enemy fire, the pilots landed 12 gliders on target and no less than 47 of the 144 in the sea. On the U.S. front, 3,400 of the paratroops reached the mainland, some being as much as 25 miles (40 km) off target and mostly in scattered parties.

OPPOSITE: A German motorcycle dispatch rider and Italian soldiers. Relationships between the German and Italian forces were often not as amicable as is suggested in such photographs.

RIGHT: British infantrymen were forced to learn the art of urban warfare in parts of the fighting for Sicily in July 1943.

The weather was rough, and although Patton's infantry got ashore successfully, there was delay in landing tanks and artillery. At that moment, with one foot in the sea and the other on land, they were violently counterattacked at Gela, in the centre of the intended beach-head. Here the Americans, especially their regular 1st Division and parties of paratroops, literally "marching to the sound of the guns," showed superb fighting spirit, stopping the Hermann Göring Division, with its 100-odd tanks, just short of the beach, aided by some astonishingly accurate fire from the guns of the U.S. Navy cruisers covering the landings. This dispelled any notion that the Americans could not fight, or were no match for German armored forces.

After a good start, the 8th Army then met with stiff resistance. Sicily, with its narrow roads, terraces, and sharp ridges was ideal for defense and gave a foretaste of what the Allies were to face for the next two years as they slogged north along the mainland of Italy. Montgomery was slowed down and almost halted, and Patton viewed this delay with intense impatience, eventually persuading Alexander to let his army go over to a full offensive. Once off the leash, he turned away to his left, made a remarkable dash for Palermo, captured it, and started to race Montgomery for Messina along the northern coast. He won by a short head, but the Germans, in a masterly withdrawal behind a series of defence lines, got clean away across the strait, without their equipment, but with most of the principal asset, their men, intact.

The 8th Army then hopped unopposed over the strait on September 3, and its 5th Division began to work its

LEFT: *German antitank gunners wait for a target to present itself. This is a 2.95-inch (75-mm) Pak 40 towed gun, which was one of the most formidable weapons Allied tanks had to face, its shot having the power to penetrate 4.5-inch (115-mm) armor at 545 yards (500m).*

BELOW: *The Germans handled their armored resources well in the Italian campaign, but Allied artillery and air power exacted a heavy toll wherever and whenever they could catch German tanks and self-propelled guns.*

OPPOSITE: *Salerno, September 1943. German prisoners are marched off toward waiting ships as the Allies secure their first major toehold on mainland Italy.*

way along the coast from Calabria toward Salerno, where the next act was to be performed. Operation Avalanche, at Salerno, proved to be a desperate affair. It had been preceded by the dramatic fall of Mussolini and the surrender of Italy, and the Allies vainly hoped that the Italian army might even change sides. The Germans had foreseen the danger, however, and brutally disarmed their late ally to prevent this from happening. What many soldiers thought would be a walkover therefore turned into a bloody battle.

Lieutenant-General Mark W. Clark's U.S. 5th Army, with two British and one U.S. division leading, landed smoothly enough on September 9, but the Germans were ready for them. Salerno is ringed with mountains, affording splendid observation, and between artillery fire and counterattack the invaders were pinned near the beaches; indeed, the British and Americans could not join up, and for a time no further landings could be made in the British sector. The British 56th (London) Division was driven back, and when the Panzers broke through the front of the U.S. 36th Division, they were stopped only just short of the beaches by U.S. divisional artillery fire at close range. The whole of the shallow beach-head and the beaches themselves were under

observed artillery fire, as was the fleet lying in Salerno bay under air attack from the new German guided glide-bombs. There was talk of re-embarkation, but this was sternly quashed by Alexander, who was at the beach-head. Reinforcements were landed, and two British 15-inch (381-mm) gun battleships arrived to give added fire support, U.S. heavy bombers were called in and the British 5th Division pressed up north from the toe of Italy, distracting the defense.

The German opposition began to wilt under the massive firepower which met every one of their attacks. The British and Americans began to take the offensive, pushing out the perimeter and making room for the British 7th Armoured Division to start punching along the road to Naples.

Commanding on the Italian front, Field-Marshal Albert Kesselring saw that he had to choose between being destroyed where he stood or breaking clear to fight a rearguard action, protected by an immense belt of demolitions prepared by his engineers.

He opted for the latter; not a bridge was left standing and every road was mined. He abandoned Naples and fell back slowly to his main defensive position, the "Gustav" Line. This ran from coast to coast from the mouth of the Garigliano river in the west to Ortona in the east. The Allied armies, the 5th on the left and the 8th on the right, began to advance toward this, driving in the German rearguards and outposts, a preliminary that was in itself a major task. The Germans proved masters of defensive fighting in Italy, and it was not until the 5th Army had fought one battle to cross the Volturno river and another to capture Monte Camino, that its patrols could even examine the formidable Gustav Line defenses immediately behind the Garigliano and Rapido rivers. The rivers were, in effect, the moat of this excellent defensive line, the mountains the bastions, and Monte Cassino the guard tower of the gateway through which the road led to Rome.

The fighting continued until late in December, during which period the 8th Army took Bari and Foggia, fought a

three-day battle for Termoli, and crossed the Trigno and Sangro rivers against strong resistance. They took Orsogna after three attempts and Ortona after 12 days, both occasions being notable for some savage street fighting between Canadian infantry and German paratroops. All this hard fighting on the Adriatic coast wore the Germans down but was strategically useless, for behind each ridge and river was another just as doggedly held. The solution, the Allies felt, was to use their sea-power for yet another landing to outflank the Gustav Line positions and open the road to Rome. The site chosen for this "Shingle" undertaking was Anzio. If the 5th Army could break through the western end of the Gustav Line and the force landed at Anzio could cut inland, the right wing of the German 10th Army might well be trapped and destroyed. The problem was how to break through the line. An attempt early in January 1944 to cross the Garigliano and Rapido rivers failed dismally. It was then decided that the correct strategy was to force a passage through the Cassino gap along Highway

6 to Rome, but that this would not be possible until Monte Cassino itself had been taken. Accordingly, on January 22, Major-General John P. Lucas, commanding the U.S. VI Corps, landed single British and U.S. divisions on the beaches at Anzio, and on January 24 Major-General Geoffrey Keyes launched his U.S. II Corps at the Cassino defenses.

Lucas has been blamed for not immediately advancing after his successful landing, so creating confusion in the rear of the Gustav Line, but military historians now agree that this would have been folly. The Germans are rightly celebrated for the speed and aggression of their reactions to the unexpected, and if Kesselring had been

able to cut in behind to sever its line of communications, the VI Corps would have been helpless for lack of supplies. Lucas wisely paused to secure his beach-head and base, but in doing so was to be besieged for four months. Kesselring had been fully prepared for such a landing. His first move was to send batteries of 3.465-inch (88-mm) dual-purpose guns, from the air defense of Rome, to form a screen of antitank guns around Anzio, the simultaneous issuing of a single codeword launching pre-warned elements of the German reserves, racing down Italy, to form a perimeter defence. These were followed by a division from France and another from Yugoslavia, three regiments from Germany itself, and two heavy tank battalions. Thus, by the time the Royal Navy and the U.S. Navy had, with exemplary speed, unloaded Lucas's formations and he was ready to attack with four divisions, Kesselring had assembled eight divisions to block him. The result was that far from being able to break out and help the 5th Army, Lucas was subjected to powerful counteroffensives which threatened to destroy his position. With his 14th Army containing the beach-head, and the 10th comfortably holding off both the 8th and

the 5th Armies, Kesselring was well placed. The VI Corps, however, stood firm, and never looked like being beaten. Lucas himself was vindicated by events, and was very unfairly dismissed when the crisis was over. In the meantime, Alexander felt it essential to help Lucas by making a full-scale attack, and onJanuary 24 the U.S. II Corps began the first of the four battles for Cassino.

Monte Cassino is the name of a spur, crowned by the ancient monastery overlooking Highway 6, its intricate defensive system, garrisoned by three battalions of paratroops, embracing a whole group of peaks. Any attacking force had first to fight its way over the Rapido river, past the town, and then climb 1,500 feet (460m) under fire, first to locate and then to assault the cunningly sited German positions in the crags and gullies behind the crest, from which came streams of interlocking machine-gun fire. It was not possible for the Americans to deploy their massive fire support or their tanks in this situation, so the issue had to be decided by close combat. The U.S. 34th Division and the Moroccans and Algerians of the French Expeditionary Corps reached the crest-line and battled there for 18 days, reaching a point within 1,100 yards (1000m) of the great Benedictine monastery; but a kilometer is a very

ABOVE LEFT: *German soldiers surrender to U.S. infantrymen.*

LEFT: *The armistice, which the Italians had secretly signed with the Allies on September 3, came into effect on September 9, just as the Allies had begun to land at Salerno.*

OPPOSITE ABOVE: *Italian civilians read a U.S. proclamation. Most Italians, especially in the south, welcomed what they saw as an Allied liberation of Italy.*

OPPOSITE BELOW: *Numerically and tactically, the most important tank fielded by the Allies in the Italian campaign was the M4 Sherman medium tank. Such a tank is seen here, negotiating a Sicilian sand dune after coming ashore from a tank landing craft.*

long way in mountain warfare. This first attempt ended only after the U.S. battalions had lost three-quarters of their fighting strength, which were replaced by the New Zealand 2nd and Indian 4th Divisions.

After much discussion, it was decided to attack the monastery directly, and the highly controversial decision was taken to use heavy bombers to blast open the German defenses. Major-General F.I.S. Tuker, an experienced Indian Army officer, urged a widely circling attack in the higher ground, in which his skilled mountain troops would bypass the monastery defenses, but this was disregarded. Bombing had no effect, for the buildings themselves were not occupied, and after two days the New Zealand commander, Lieutenant-General Sir Bernard Freyberg, stopped the attacks.

On March 15 he started them again, this time asking for Cassino town to be bombed, but this also had little effect except to create a miniature Stalingrad, where Panzergrenadiers and New Zealanders fought at close quarters in the ruins. No attempt was made to coordinate bombardments with attacks, the defenders repeating their fathers' tactics of the Western Front, by going to ground in the impregnable rock and concrete shelters, to pop out and man

their weapons when the bombing stopped and the assaulting troops appeared. Every scrap of food, can of water, and box of ammunition for the attackers, had to be carried up by hand, and when not fighting, the attackers were obliged to defend their gains under continuous artillery fire, causing a steady loss of men.

As Tuker had foreseen, it had been useless to attack the Germans at their strongest point. The Indian engineers brought off the extraordinary feat of building a secret track up the mountain.

It was fit for tanks, and a squadron drove up it, but to no avail.

Freyberg persisted for three weeks, by which time he had lost 4,000 men. The offensive was finally halted on March 23, the forward troops were pulled back, and the ground won consolidated. Both sides now paused to rest and recover. Each soldier was mentally and physically exhausted by the cold, the wet, the ceaseless bombardments, and the strain of months of bitter fighting. Alexander, advised by his chief of staff, Lieutenant-General Alan F.J. Harding, decided to rest and regroup his troops until the spring, when the advent of better weather and dry ground would allow him to use his two primary assets: armour and warplanes. Alexander would then launch a properly co-ordinated offensive, at the same time using all his resources to break through the Gustav Line with a single concentrated punch, at the same time advancing with maximum possible force from the beach-head at Anzio. This, he felt sure, would break the deadlock. It would be better still if he could destroy the bulk of the 10th Army, where they stood facing him in southern Italy, thus opening up the whole peninsula to a rapid Allied advance to the north. This great operation, since it was to set the crown on a year of hard fighting, was to be called Diadem.

WORLD WAR II

Chapter Three
THE GERMANS ARE EXPELLED FROM THE USSR

The rapid pace and wide geographical extent of their efforts in 1943 cost the Soviet forces very dearly. Many hundreds of thousands of men were lost, and tanks, guns, aircraft, and other war matériel had been expended at a prodigious rate. But as a result of the efforts of its growing armaments industry, in the area east of the Urals, the USSR was able not only to resupply its armies, but also to equip, on a relatively lavish scale, the new formations that were also being brought into existence in large numbers. Hitler had gambled on a quick war, so that the USSR's resources in industry and manpower should not be used to their full extent, and had lost. No matter how great the casualties inflicted on the Soviet forces, the Germans could not

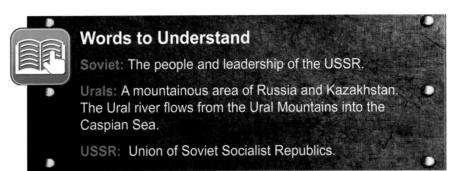

Words to Understand

Soviet: The people and leadership of the USSR.

Urals: A mountainous area of Russia and Kazakhstan. The Ural river flows from the Ural Mountains into the Caspian Sea.

USSR: Union of Soviet Socialist Republics.

destroy enough to force the USSR out of the war. The Soviets fought in a tactical manner which was relatively unsophisticated, exploiting the availability of their supplies of the right types of weapon, such as the excellent T-34 tank, and the commanders were

prepared to expend the lives of large numbers of men. Germany, on the other hand, could not do this: its armies fought a tactically advanced type of warfare, using the latest weapons, but it could not keep up with the losses inflicted by the Soviets, and although in 1943–44 its armies were still of a superior quality to those of the Soviets, this was more than counterbalanced by the enormously superior quantity of the Soviet forces. Supplied by the Americans and British with considerable war matériel, including large numbers of trucks, the Soviets were gradually developing a characteristic pattern of hard-hitting, fast mobile warfare,

LEFT: The Germans made excellent use of captured equipment of all types. The Marder self-propelled antitank gun, for example, was the Germans' own 2.95-inch (75-mm) Pak 40 antitank gun on a limited-traverse mounting on the hull of the Czechoslovak LT-38 tank, which had been used as a gun tank earlier in the war with the designation PzKpfw 38(t).

OPPOSITE: Throughout the latter part of World War II, the Germans revealed themselves to be masters of defensive warfare. Here German troops rip up a railroad track as they pull back on the Eastern Front.

admirably suited to their armies and the terrain of the western USSR. With supply outstripping demand, the Soviets were able to keep up an almost non-stop offensive, with fresh troops always ready to take over from exhausted formations.

In 1941 Hitler had ordered Field-Marshal Wilhelm von Leeb's Army Group North not to take Leningrad by direct assault, but rather to invest the city and destroy it by starvation and bombardment. The investment had been completed when von Leeb's forces reached the southern shore of Lake Ladoga, joining the ring of Axis forces around the birthplace of the USSR with the Finnish hold on the region to the north. Leningrad's trials in the following months were appalling, with thousands dying of starvation every day, and disease and cold taking their toll. It is estimated that the people of Leningrad were dying at the rate of 20,000 every day by the end of 1943. Nevertheless, the city continued to hold off the German forces.

Supplies were brought in over the frozen surface of Lake Ladoga, during the winter of 1941–42, but this, of course, ended with the thaw in March 1942, when conditions deteriorated rapidly. In August 1942, the Leningrad and Volkhov Fronts launched a joint offensive, with the aim of cutting the corridor from Tosno north to Lake Ladoga, held by the German 18th Army, but this failed and Leningrad remained under siege. An attempt to link up with the forces locked up at Oranienbaum, farther to the west along the Gulf of Finland, also failed at the same time. In January 1943, however, hope of eventual relief appeared when the Leningrad and Volkhov Fronts finally managed to cut their way through to just south of Lake Ladoga and link up near Sinyavino. Although this "Corridor of Death" was under constant threat by German artillery, a trickle of supplies reached Leningrad, and German efforts to cut the Soviet land bridge failed. The limits of this supply route precluded the total relief of the city, which lost perhaps 1 million people during the siege, but it did prevent conditions from worsening.

Almost exactly a year after the link to Leningrad had been opened, the Soviets at last managed to free the city from the constant threat of German conquest. At the same time, they drove the forces of Army Group North, commanded by Field-Marshal Georg von Küchler, back to Lake Peipus in Estonia. On January 15, 1944 the forces of the Leningrad and Volkhov Fronts, commanded by Generals L.A. Govorov and K.A. Meretskov respectively, swept forward, catching the Germans com-pletely off their guard. The Leningrad Front crossed the frozen Gulf of Finland, falling on the left of the German 18th Army, commanded by General Georg Lindemann, while the Volkhov Front crossed the frozen lakes and marshes further to the south to attack the 18th Army's right. By the end of the year, the Soviets had advanced to the line of the Luga river and had taken the historic capital of the area, Novgorod. Lindemann pulled his army back and just evaded encirclement. The

2nd Baltic Front, under General M.M. Popov, had made limited attacks still farther to the south, but in February began a major offensive to advance the Soviet front line to the line running along the Velikaya river south from Pskov, at the southern end of Lake Peipus. When the thaw began at the beginning of March, bringing hostilities to a temporary halt, Field-Marshal Walther Model, who had replaced von Küchler on January 29, had only just managed to begin to check the Soviets. The German threat to Leningrad had at last been removed after the greatest siege of modern times.

Meanwhile, in the south, the Soviets had been continuing their offensive against the Germans in Ukraine. Supported on its right by Colonel-General P.A. Kurochkin's 2nd Belorussian Front, on December 24, 1943 the 1st Ukrainian Front, under General N.F. Vatutin, struck west in a great offensive from its bridgehead around Kiev. General I.S. Konev's 2nd Ukrainian Front also moved onto the offensive farther to the south, between Kanev and Kirovograd, on January 5, 1944, with General R.Y. Malinovsky's 3rd Ukrainian Front and General F.I.

Tolbukhin's 4th Ukrainian Front, on each side of Zaporozhye at the head of the Dniepr bend, joining the offensive on January 10 and 11 respectively. There was nothing the Germans could do but try to extricate themselves as best they could. Field-Marshal Erich von Manstein's Army Group South and Field-Marshal Ewald von Kleist's Army Group A tried to stem the Soviet winter advance, but lacked the strength to halt the vast Soviet fronts. On January 29, two corps were trapped at Korsun-Shevchenkovsky, and although von Manstein immediately set about putting together a relief force, a major part of the two corps had been lost, together with all the divisions' heavy equipment, by the time the relief force and the cut-off garrison met on February 17. Von Manstein's efforts had been greatly hampered by atrocious winter conditions and the overall exhaustion of his men.

The Soviets continued to grind forward right into April, despite the brilliance of many counterattacks mounted by the indefatigable von Manstein, who yet again demonstrated his remarkable tactical genius. In the confusion of such operations, it was hardly surprising that another German

army was now cut off. This was the 1st Panzerarmee, commanded by General Hans Hube. Isolated to the east of Kamenets Podolskiy on March 10, Hube prevented his forces from being pinned down by the superior Soviet armies opposing him. Keeping constantly on the move, and supplied from the air, the 1st Panzerarmee fought a brilliant battle against the Soviet lines of communication, as ordered by von Manstein, who kept a close personal supervision over the whole operation by radio. Unable to pin down this highly mobile force, the Soviets were at a loss to know what to do, slowing their advance in the area. Finally Hube turned west, and in conjunction with an attack south from Tarnopol, by the 4th Panzerarmee, now commanded by Colonel-General Erhard Raus, broke out through the Soviet front line, keeping his forces almost intact.

Yet the Soviets were still moving steadily forward. Commanded by more than competent generals, and supervised from Moscow by Marshal Georgi Zhukov and Josef Stalin, who kept a personal link open to all senior commanders, the Soviets seemed invincible. Despite the tactical genius of their commanders and their own skill and determination, the German soldiers were outnumbered and driven back. History shows that von Kleist conducted an exemplary retreat, and von Manstein a brilliant one, but Hitler dismissed both of these commanders on March 30. Colonel-General Ferdinand Schörner, a hard-line Nazi but adequate general, took command of von Kleist's Army Group South Ukraine (ex-Army Group A) and Field-Marshal Walther Model became commander of von Manstein's Army Group North Ukraine (ex-Army Group South).

Vatutin was killed in March and was succeeded on April 1 by Zhukov, and the Soviets pressed forward. The German 6th and 8th Armies in the south were badly mauled, and the great Black Sea port of Odessa fell on April 10. By the middle of the month, the Soviets had cleared the Axis forces out of the whole of the USSR to the south of the Pripyet marshes. The Soviet forces had crossed the Bug, Dniestr, and Prut rivers, and the Ukrainian fronts were now deep into southern Poland and northern Romania. Trapped in Crimea, the German 17th Army was faced with the impossible task of holding off the 2nd Guards and 51st Armies of Tolbukhin's 4th Ukrainian Front, which attacked south along the Perekop isthmus on 8 April, and General A.I. Eremenko's Independent Coastal Army, which crossed from the Taman peninsula into the Kerch peninsula on April 11. The 17th Army was driven back towards Sevastopol, from which only a few men could be evacuated. Hitler had insisted that Crimea be held as a jumping-off point for the reconquest of the southern USSR, and his increasing refusal to see the realities of the situation cost Germany the fine 17th Army when the last parts of Sevastopol fell on May 12.

The winter and spring campaigns had cleared the southern USSR, and Stalin now planned to use the summer offensive to clear the central USSR and Belorussia, just to the north of the Pripyet marshes. The offensive was entrusted, from south to north, to Marshal K.K. Rokossovsky's 1st Belorussian, Colonel-General M.V. Zakharov's 2nd Belorussian, Colonel-General I.D. Chernyakovsky's 3rd Belorussian and Colonel-General I.K. Bagramyan's 1st Baltic Fronts. These four had as their primary task the destruction of Field-Marshal Ernst Busch's Army Group Center. The offensive was to be launched from the area just to the west of

Smolensk and Gomel, the axis being west toward East Prussia. As usual, immediate overall command of the whole operation was entrusted to Zhukov, by now deputy supreme commander of the Soviet armed forces under Stalin. Mustering some 400 guns per mile (250 guns per kilometer), the four Soviet fronts began their offensive against the hapless Army Group Centre after a devastating barrage on June 23. Disorganized at the front by the Soviet artillery and in its rear areas by the ever-increasing activities of Soviet partisans, now a formidable force, Army Group Center could not even retreat before the armored offensive. The Soviets smashed a 250-mile (400-km) gap through the German front, and through this poured massed armor and infantry. The Soviet air forces had total command of the air, and the armor drove forward as swiftly as possible, leaving the infantry to mop up and follow on as best it could. As usual, Hitler expressly forbade retreat, ordering cut-off formations to stand and fight until relieved, even though there were no relief forces to be had. The Soviets retook Vitebsk on June 25, Bobruysk on June 27 and Minsk on July 3. For the first time in the war, an entire German army group had been destroyed: 25 of Busch's 33 divisions had been cut off and destroyed, and

the Soviets claimed to have killed 400,000 Germans, captured 158,000, and destroyed or taken 2,000 armored vehicles, 10,000 guns, and 57,000 vehicles.

The loss of Belorussia and the destruction of Army Group Center, which had been completed by July 4, was a catastrophe of incalculable proportions for the Germans, yet the size of the forces deployed by the Soviets cannot detract from Zhukov's genius in planning and controlling such a successful and speedy campaign. Busch was almost inevitably dismissed by Hitler, who entrusted command of the shattered Army Group Center to Model, who also kept command of Army Group North Ukraine.

This was only the first stage of the Soviet summer offensive. The Belorussian fronts continued westward, taking Vilnyus on July 13, Brest-Litovsk on July 28, and reaching the outskirts of Warsaw by the end of August. Colonel-General Georg-Hans Reinhardt, previously commander of the 3rd Panzerarmee, badly mauled near Vitebsk, succeeded Model as head of Army Group Center on August 16 when Model left for France, where the situation was worsening after the Allied break-out from their Normandy lodgement. Model's position as

commander of Army Group North Ukraine passed to Colonel-General Josef Harpe, although he was only confirmed in this post after the army group had become Army Group A during September.

No amount of reordering of already shattered commands and forces could halt the Soviets, however. On July 13 Konev's 1st Ukrainian Front, just to the south of the 1st Belorussian Front, had gone over to the offensive, and was joined still farther to the south on August 5 by General I.E. Petrov's 4th Ukrainian Front, only recently formed. By the end of August, the Ukrainian and Belorussian fronts had reached a north and south line running from Jaslo in southern Poland, past the east of Warsaw, around East Prussia and thence into Lithuania. The advance since the end of July had been small, for the Soviets had advanced some 450 miles (725km) and their lines of communications could no longer sustain further advance.

Yet just as the Soviets began to slow at the beginning of August, there occurred one of the most remarkable and heroic actions of the war. In Warsaw the Polish Home Army had for long been secretly planning a rising against the German garrison, once the Soviets were within reach of the city. Despite their anti-Communist feelings, the men of the Home Army, under the command of General Tadeusz Bor-Komorowski, rose against the Germans on August 1. The 1st Belorussian Front had recently halted, just over the Vistula river from Warsaw, possibly to ensure that this non-Communist Polish armed force would be defeated, and after a hopeless but heroic defense the Home Army was crushed in bitter fighting by the end of September. What was left of Warsaw after the German campaign of 1939, and the reduction of the Jewish ghetto after this, was almost totally destroyed in the vicious two-month campaign by the SS.

On July 4 General A.I. Eremenko's 2nd Baltic Front, General I.I. Maslennikov's 3rd Baltic Front, and General L.A. Govorov's Leningrad Front extended the Soviet general offensive to the north. Together with the 1st Baltic

and 3rd Belorussian Fronts, they swept into the Baltic states, occupied by the USSR in 1940, and lost to the Germans in 1941. Army Group North, commanded by Colonel-General Georg Lindemann, was unable to stem the Soviet advance and fell back toward the Baltic. Although this army group was threatened by the distinct possibility of being cut off by the Belorussian fronts' advance toward East Prussia, Hitler again would not even consider the possibility of retreat. Forced back from the line of the Narva and Velikaya rivers, Army Group North eventually found itself in western Latvia, where it was cut off in the peninsula north of a line between Tukums, on the Bay of Riga, and Liepaja on the Baltic Sea, when the forces of the 1st Baltic Front reached the sea on October 10. Narva had fallen on July 26, Daugavpils (Dvinsk) on July 27, Kaunas on August 1 and the bastion of Riga was to fall on October 15. Colonel-General Heinz Guderian, who had replaced Colonel-General Kurt Zeitzler as OKH chief of staff, was appalled by Hitler's decision to allow this important and powerful force to be locked up by the Soviets, where it would be paralyzed to further Germany's war aims. The men of Army Group North remained trapped and useless in the Kurland peninsula right up to the end of the war, although some units were evacuated by ships of the German navy.

With the threat to Leningrad now removed, the Soviets were able to turn their attention in this region to Finland. In the middle of June, five Soviet armies attacked north-west along the Karelian isthmus and around each end of Lake Onega, and after at first being halted by a skilful Finnish defense, began to make ground. The Mannerheim Line was finally breached, and on June 20 the Soviet forces took Viipuri. Seeing the hopelessness of their position, the Finns sued for and were granted an armistice on September 4, under the terms of which the Finns had to clear their former co-belligerents, the Germans, out of the country; there was some sharp fighting before this was accomplished. In the far north, on the shores of the Arctic, the German 20th Army was driven back out of the USSR by Meretskov's Karelian Front in October, and the Soviets eventually pushed on into Norway, although the little ports of Petsamo and Kirkenes were able to hold out.

The Soviet advances in northern Ukraine and Belorussia had by now placed Army Group South Ukraine, now commanded by Colonel-General Johannes Friessner, in a difficult position. Any Soviet advance into southern Poland and Hungary would threaten it with being cut off, together with Army Groups E and F in Greece and Yugoslavia respectively, especially if Hitler refused permission to pull back, which seemed likely. The Soviets saw this as clearly as the Germans, and launched an attack into Romania on August 20 with the 2nd and 3rd Ukrainian Fronts. The German 6th and Romanian 3rd Armies were quickly trapped, the Soviets pressing on to the Danube river by August 29. Romania, long disaffected with the Axis cause by lack of success, capitulated on August 23, declaring war on Germany two days later. The Romanian 3rd and 4th Armies quickly joined with the Soviets to press the campaign against their former allies. Reaching the Romanian capital on August 31, the Soviets wheeled west and then north-west to drive into southern Hungary. By September 24 Romania had been entirely overrun.

The 37th and 57th Armies of the 3rd Ukrainian Front continued south-west, however, plunging into Bulgaria, which surrendered on September 4, and joining the USSR four days later. Beset by partisans and the Bulgarian 1st Army, Army Group E succeeded in pulling back from Greece to link with Army Group F in Yugoslavia. Greatly weakened by the loss of much of the 6th and 8th Armies, Army Group South Ukraine nonetheless attempted to hold

southern Hungary, with Army Groups E and F to its right in Yugoslavia. It was an impossible task, and the Soviets moved with ease into Hungary and eastern Yugoslavia where, with the aid of the now-considerable partisan forces of Marshal Tito, they took Belgrade on October 19. By the end of 1944, the Soviets were firmly ensconced in the Balkans, ready to drive forward into Austria and Czechoslovakia.

The USSR had been cleared. Finland, Romania, and Bulgaria had dropped out of the war, the latter two then rejoining it on the other side. The Soviet armies were poised to sweep into the territories bordering Germany and thence into Germany proper. Stalin had every reason to be pleased with the performance of his forces. All Germany could do, given a leadership which refused even the notion of asking for terms, was to fight on desperately in the hope of slowing the Soviets, who were still to have a hard time of it in 1945.

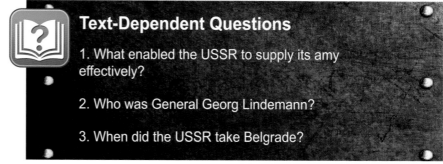

Text-Dependent Questions

1. What enabled the USSR to supply its amy effectively?

2. Who was General Georg Lindemann?

3. When did the USSR take Belgrade?

Research Projects

What are the main resons why German lost the war with the USSR?

WORLD WAR II

Chapter Four
BREAKING THE GUSTAV LINE AND THE RETURN TO FRANCE

There is a fascinating reversal of thinking to be found in American and British attitudes to the way in which the war would be fought in South-East Asia and Italy. With regard to Burma and China, the U.S. leadership favored an offensive strategy and felt that the British were dragging their feet, while the British saw no merit in becoming entangled in the mountains and jungles of upper Burma to help China, which was an ally of only doubtful capability, when they were free to strike farther to the south and east by sea. By contrast, the British felt that, in Italy, they already had a foothold in Europe and wished to exploit it without risking all on the hazardous cross-Channel crossing desired by the Americans. Prime Minister Winston Churchill, always a great exponent of the "indirect approach," envisaged a wide movement into Austria and central Europe and so into southern Germany. The Americans were, as always, against this on the grounds that it was not the direct approach to the main enemy as mandated by their military philosophy: Operation Overlord against Normandy and the direct approach was their choice, followed by another landing, Operation Dragoon, in the south of France. In addition, General Sir Harold Alexander in Italy was to transfer seven divisions immediately for Overlord, and another six later in 1944 for Dragoon. His role was limited to keeping as many German divisions as possible occupied in Italy.

Alexander supported Churchill's strategy but commanded a multi-national army group: his second-in-command was a U.S. officer, one of his armies was American, and one corps was French. Moreover, the French wanted desperately to fight to liberate France herself, not any other country. Alexander decided, therefore, that the most effective way to carry out his mission was to fix his eyes on the Po valley, the Julian Alps, and the Ljubljana gap in Yugoslavia leading to central Europe, driving there as hard as he could with all his force. Although he was comparatively weak in divisions, he had command of the air, overwhelming resources in weapons, and all the advantages in support services including, most importantly of all, engineers to build bridges. A remorseless drive to the north would keep his opponent as busy as any other more cautious and limited offensives. Such was the background of the Italian campaign in 1944, which saw the commitment of more troops (some 40 divisions on the two sides) than in any theater, other than that of the Eastern Front.

Alexander felt that his first task was to reorganize his armies and then to launch Diadem for the solution of the Cassino-Anzio stalemate. The plan was to let operations die down on the Adriatic coast and shift the British 8th Army to the center. Some military experts believe that the secret of

LEFT: *The German defense of southern Italy, especially at Cassino, was synonymous with the great tenacity and fighting skills of the elite German parachute divisions. Here are paratroopers in Rome, before the Italian capital was declared an open city and abandoned to the Allies in June 1944.*

OPPOSITE ABOVE: *British armor approaches the German Gothic Line defenses in northern Italy.*

OPPOSITE BELOW: *British Churchill infantry tanks on the move in open country.*

mountain warfare is to avoid it, as it offers endless opportunities for delaying action. The new effort was to be made along the Rapido valley below Cassino, to burst through into the Liri valley. The British XIII Corps, under Lieutenant-General Sidney C. Kirkman, in Montgomery's opinion the best artillery officer in the British army, had the leading role with one armored division, three infantry divisions and 1,000 guns, followed by the Canadian I Corps of one armored and one infantry division, its task being to bridge the Rapido river and break into the valley defenses under cover of a dense and prolonged smokescreen. This lasted from 12–18 May and used 813 tons of smoke munitions and 135,000 artillery smoke shells alone. Altogether, something approaching 1 million shells of all kinds were fired. The German batteries

received a barrage of seven tons of heavy shells in a few minutes, and when the Canadians attacked the rear edge of the Gustav Line, known as the "Hitler" Line, their preliminary bombardment was at the rate of 1,000 shells an hour.

This vast mass of artillery was to switch to the Cassino heights as necessary, to support two Polish divisions, who were to clear the heights once and for all. On the left of the Liri valley the French Expeditionary Corps, with single Algerian and Moroccan colonial divisions, all experienced mountaineers, was to clear the heights on the left with startling success, while the U.S. II Corps was to attack near the coast. Then, at the appropriate moment, one U.S. armored, three U.S. infantry and two British divisions were to mount an offensive from the Anzio beach-head and make for Valmonte. As before, their

task was to cut Highway 6 and trap the German divisions as they were being driven back from the Gustav Line. The RAF and USAAF were to concentrate on attacking the German reserves as they were moved up, and also on giving close air support to the advancing troops, using new and highly-developed methods of communication from ground to air.

Altogether 41 divisions were involved in this great battle: eight German encircling Anzio; ten in the crucial area of the Gustav Line; six Allied in the Anzio beach-head; and 17 between Cassino and the sea. Diadem was thus a great battle, and one which could have been decisive. Although it was a resounding success, it was excluded from the news and public notice by the launching of Overlord, on June 6, just after the Gustav Line

ABOVE: The Allied armies, by the closing stages of the Italian campaign, had great matériel superiority over the Germans, especially in artillery and, in general, the ammunition needed for it. Here, British artillery is engaged in the fighting for the Gothic Line.

OPPOSITE: General Sir Bernard Montgomery with his senior officers at Eighth Army Headquarters at Vasto, shortly before handing over command of the Eighth Army to General Sir Oliver Leese and leaving Italy to prepare for the Normandy invasion in England.

defenses had collapsed, before just failing to achieve complete victory. This was due in part to the courage and tenacity of the Germans, who refused to admit defeat: they extricated their savaged battle groups, formed rearguards, and in spite of the unceasing attacks of the Allied air forces, retreated in order up through Italy to their next main position in the Apennines, namely the Gothic Line. The other cause was a decision by Clark to vary his orders. Resulting from national pride, personal vanity, or a belief that it was politically and strategically important to capture Rome, Clark's decision has long been the subject of controversy. Leaving only one division to follow the thrust line laid down by Alexander, he swung four U.S. divisions away to the left. He was held up along an intermediate Caesar Line, and it can be argued that had this been allowed to solidify there would have been a long delay if Clark had not broken through it; but there can be no doubt that he had departed from his orders, and the delicacy of Alexander's position was that Clark was allowed to get away with it. As a result the 10th Army escaped.

One of the surprises of the battle was the success of General Alphonse Juin's French-African troops. These were sent into the rugged and roadless mountain sector between the Americans and the British XIII Corps, more or less to keep the Germans in that sector occupied. Juin first infiltrated his infantry, capturing a vital peak which

The Gustav Line is Broken

controlled the Liri valley on the south side, as Cassino did on the north. Then, using his *goumiers* (irregular Moroccan mounted infantry), Juin cut through the Gustav Line, came out behind it and caused the defenses of the German left flank to collapse, while the British and Canadian armored divisions, choked with their abundant transport, were still stuck in traffic jams in the Liri valley. Had this been foreseen, or exploited when it happened, the battle might have turned out very differently.

On the other side of the valley, it cost the Poles 4,000 casualties to capture the Cassino heights. Thus the defense of the position, by Major-General Richard Heidrich and his paratroops, cost the Allies altogether some 12,000 casualties, the battle remaining one of the epics of defensive warfare. It was fitting that the Germans should be overcome by their deadliest enemies: on May 18 the 12th Podolski Lancers, fighting as infantry,

raised the Polish flag over the ruins of the monastery.

If Alexander had achieved nothing else he had fulfilled his mission of drawing in reserves. By June 6, D-Day for Overlord, four divisions had been sent to Kesselring to prevent a total collapse of the German position in Italy and later he was to be given three more. The result was that when the battle to pierce the Gothic Line began, Alexander's numerical superiority had changed to an adverse balance of 20 to 22. However, in air power, weapons and supplies he still had a great advantage. He began his campaign against Kesselring's rearguards as soon as the confusion of the breakthrough and the 5th Army's change of course could be cleared up.

The advancing Allies found that every bridge had been blown, every verge and detour mined, and everything attractive booby-trapped. For the troops

for a concentrated punch effort up the coast with the Polish and Canadian corps. The main thrust would come from the British V Corps, with four divisions, some 10 miles (16km) inland through the foothills, with the aim of setting the armor loose in the Po valley behind Kesselring's eastern flank. This was to commence on August 25. Hoping that after two weeks most of Kesselring's reserves would have been attracted to the east, the 5th Army was to attack the Futa and Il Giogo passes, north of Florence, early in September. A great deal of care was taken to conceal the 8th Army's concentration, around its point of main effort, by the elaborate pretence of a buildup in the center. The first attacks, by Major-General Sir John Hawkesworth, commanding the 46th Division, made in silence and without any preliminary air bombardment or covering fire, were a rapid success. To begin with, his division, with the Indian 4th Division on its left, crossed the Metauro river and attacked outposts manned by the German 71st Division, which were driven back in panic. By the end of August the whole of the 8th Army was hard up against the main German position, its patrols looking at hillsides converted to bare slopes, houses knocked down, trees and vines cleared to provide fields of fire, fields of antipersonnel and antitank mines, and the villages turned into machine-gun strongpoints. What looked to be impregnable was pierced, not simply by the weight of fire but by infantry fighting.

On September 10 it was the turn of the 5th Army to attack the fortified passes through the Apennines. Monte Altuzzo, commanding the Giglio pass and very heavily defended, was taken by the 1st Battalion, 338th Infantry Regiment, which lost 250 out of 400 men. All the heroism availed nought, for Alexander ran out of infantry reserves. The hope of a tank breakthrough on the east flank was vain. The British 1st Armoured Division was thrown repeatedly into action against their old foe, the German 3.465-inch (88-mm) antitank guns: at Ceriano the Bays of the 2nd Armoured Brigade were shot to pieces in a few minutes, the division

who had fought through the Gustav Line there was none of the excitement of a triumphant advance. All through the hot, dusty Italian summer the long columns of tanks and lorries rumbled forward, hit the enemy, stopped, patrolled, positioned the artillery, and attacked uphill through the terraced fields and orchards, only to find the Germans gone. They then had to form up again, advance to the next ridge, and start all over again. In August, eventually, they began to close up onto the Gothic Line.

North of Florence the Apennines lie diagonally across Italy, offering a natural line of defense from Spezia to Pesaro, and this had been enormously strengthened by the German engineers. The route through the center was via two mountain passes. Going around the Adriatic flank meant crossing seven river valleys with 12 more rivers barring

the way in the wide valley of the Po. It was a battle demanding vast resources as well as good tactics. Good military plans are usually very simple. All they require is first-class staff work and a combination of good troops, reserves and weather. The first was assured, although some of the best divisions were very tired, the second was non-existent, and the third was not going to last for more than a few weeks. Kesselring's veterans were equally tired and depleted, but they had been reinforced with fresh troops and their defenses were ready. As things stood there was no question of a quick Allied breakthrough and there was little chance of exploitation should one be achieved, but Alexander and his army commanders decided to try.

The plan, suggested by Lieutenant-General Sir Oliver Leese, who had taken Montgomery's place, was for the 8th Army to be moved back to the Adriatic

eventually having to be disbanded. The 8th Army lost 14,000 men killed, wounded, and missing. It had advanced 30 miles (48km), losing 200 tanks on the way and now it was stuck. Moreover, it had begun to rain.

At one moment it looked as if the 5th Army, having cleared the passes, might almost have cracked the position open in the center: there were only another 15 miles (24km) to go and from the forward positions Bologna could just be seen in the plain far below. At that desperate moment even Kesselring himself thought he had lost, but rain, mud, bad flying weather and the defense, stopped the 5th Army's infantry in the mountains just as it had stopped the 8th Army's armour in the plain.

OPPOSITE: Sherman tanks advance during the assault on the Gustav Line at Cassino, Italy. May 15, 1944.

ABOVE: Germany's Atlantic Wall defenses included sizeable numbers of large-caliber guns emplaced in huge concrete casemates, making them proof against heavy bombs.

RIGHT: Men of a U.S. gliderborne infantry regiment await their arrival in France during the early hours of June 6, 1944.

OPERATION OVERLORD

The Allied invasion of north-west France, across the English Channel, was the most critical and the most dangerous operation of World War II. It was critical because it opened the only route by which the military strength of the USA could be brought to bear on Germany to end the war quickly. It was dangerous, because in an amphibious operation failure is complete. This Operation Overlord was the core of Allied strategy and all possible resources were concentrated for it. So far the Allies three assault landings in the western theater, in Sicily, at Salerno, and at Anzio, against relatively weak opposition and on an unfortified coast, had been close-run things. In France, by contrast, a complete German army group, commanded by Field-Marshal Erwin Rommel, awaited the invasion with 32 divisions ready to intervene, three more in the Netherlands, and another 13 divisions of another army group in the south of France. The vulnerable parts of the French coast were defended by the Atlantic Wall, a formidable belt of obstacles and minefields covered by batteries of guns in concrete emplacements. The disastrous

Dieppe raid of August 1942, in which the Canadian 2nd Division had been very severely mauled, had shown just how different breaching the Atlantic Wall would be from landing on an Italian beach or a Pacific atoll.

For logistical reasons the largest force landed by the Allies in the first wave was five divisions, with six more to follow when there was room for them to deploy. All possible scientific and military ingenuity, therefore, had to be devoted to solving three very difficult problems: firstly, to put the assault troops safely ashore in the face of intense fire; secondly, to get tanks and artillery over the ditches and tank-traps barring the way inland; and thirdly, to supply the two armies which would pour into the beach-head, and bring in over the beaches the vast amounts of fuel, ammunition and food needed. New methods and new weapons had to be invented for the battle of the beach-head.

It was planned to saturate the entire defense system with bombing and naval bombardment, but experience taught that, however heavy a bombardment may be, enough men and weapons would survive to decimate the

attackers, so close support for the actual run-in to the beach had to be provided. This was achieved by putting armored self-propelled artillery and also multiple-rocket launchers in the landing craft. The guns then rolled ashore to give normal support until the rest of the ordinary artillery was landed. Large numbers of battle tanks were fitted with "DD" flotation gear, a British invention which enabled them to swim ashore to fight with the first wave. No less important was the part played by the tanks adapted for special jobs in the physical breaching of the defenses and operated by assault engineers. These carried super-heavy mortars for blowing up concrete bunkers, flail equipment to explode minefields, and rolls of matting, fascines, ramps, and bridges to make roads inland from the beaches. Even so, the battle would be very hard, and there would be no hope of the rapid capture of a port, or ports in working order, the

defenders being certain to have rendered them unusable. Instead, it was decided to build two harbors off the invasion beaches. A fleet of old ships was steamed across and sunk in groups to provide breakwaters, and two "Mulberry" artificial harbors, made up of floating concrete cylinders, were towed across the Channel. Oil was brought ashore by pipe-line, into which tankers discharged directly.

All this was essential, not in order to win the Battle of Normandy, which was another huge problem looming ahead, but to ensure that Field-Marshals Gerd von Rundstedt (commanding in the western theater) and Rommel did not win the "Battle of the Beach-head." For both battles the Allies had two great assets. The first of these were Air Chief-Marshal Sir Arthur Tedder and General Carl Spaatz, whose RAD and USAAF had won complete command of the air and were thus in the

ABOVE: The complete air superiority of the Allies made daylight movement of German armor in Normandy a perilous undertaking, even when the armor was PzKpfw VI Tiger heavy tanks such as these.

OPPOSITE ABOVE: D-Day placed great emphasis on the capabilities of specialized British armor, such as this Churchill AVRE (Armored Vehicle Royal Engineers), an infantry tank conversion designed to undertake a host of battlefield engineering tasks.

OPPOSITE BELOW: A Sherman medium tank of a Polish armored regiment in the ruins of the Norman city of Caen.

position to help blast the armies forward, block the movement of reserves, and massacre the defeated German columns in retreat. The second was Adolf Hitler, for as a supreme commander he had now revealed himself to be an incompetent; this was for the simple reason that he regarded war as a giant game of chess, which he played on a map sitting in his various headquarters, giving futile orders no one dared to disobey. A single one of these was to lose the Germans the war in France.

The assault was led by three airborne divisions, followed by five seaborne assault divisions with tanks landing on the beaches, followed by six more divisions, with 21 more waiting in England. They were carried by 4,262 aircraft and 4,266 ships of all kinds, supported by 2,300 combat aircraft, which flew 14,600 sorties on D-Day

alone. In the weeks before D-Day the heavy coast artillery batteries, which were the main threat to the landings, were bombed out of existence and all the railways and rolling stock, which might have moved von Rundstedt's strategic reserve to the threatened point, were wrecked. Some 80,000 tons of bombs were dropped. At sea two fleets guarded the flanks of the assault force, standing by to give covering fire to the landings, while 29 flotillas of mine-sweepers cleared the Channel coast.

The targeting of the bombing campaign was carefully arranged to avoid giving away the landing site, and an elaborate deception plan was mounted to make the Germans believe that the invasion would be launched in the Pas de Calais. In fact, after a very thorough study the Allied planners had chosen the Normandy coast in the Seine Bay, a long way to the west, as the

landing place. The reasoning behind this was long and complex, but the most obvious and important consideration was, in the first wave, room to put ashore a force strong enough to resist any initial counterattack. In overall command was General Montgomery, his detailed plan involving several components. First was the paradropping or gliderborne delivery of the British 6th Airborne Division to take and hold the vital bridges over the Orne river to protect the left flank of the proposed beach-head, and of the U.S. 82nd and 101st Airborne Divisions on the extreme right for a basically similar task. The seaborne forces to be landed between the mouths of the Orne and Vire, from left to right, were the British 3rd, Canadian 3rd and British 50th Divisions, leading the assault of the British 2nd Army, and the U.S. 1st and 4th Divisions of Lieutenant-General

Omar Bradley's U.S. 1st Army. One of the most crucial roles in the whole enterprise was that of the special parties needing to land just ahead of the assault waves, at exactly the right point of the tide to blow up the underwater obstacles on the beaches.

Timing was, of course, critical, for only certain infrequent days produced the optimum conditions of moon, tide, and sunrise. As the perfect combinations only occurred at intervals, and a postponement was fraught with great difficulties, the decision faced by General Dwight D. Eisenhower, the supreme Allied commander, on June 3–4 was appalling: the weather forecast indicated gales and rough seas, with a faint improvement possible. Faced with the alternatives of postponement and the assault divisions being cut off by storm and surf when at their most vulnerable, Eisenhower courageously opted for D-Day on June 6. The storms had not altogether abated and the bad weather hampered the landings, but it had also led the defenders to relax their vigilance.

Early that morning the airborne troops landed, and at half tide the assault divisions landed under cover of a barrage along the beaches. The naval forces stood in to pound the coastal artillery casemates and radars one last time, and 2,000 aircraft attacked the

ABOVE: *"Omaha" Beach, the most difficult of the Allied assault areas on June 6, 1944, is where the men of the U.S. 1st Infantry Division had a difficult and bloody time landing and then breaking though the German coastal defenses.*

OPPOSITE ABOVE: *"Utah" Beach was on the extreme right of the Allied assault on D-Day, and is where the U.S. 4th Infantry Division landed, then drove inland to link up with the previously landed men of the U.S. 82nd and 101st Airborne Divisions.*

OPPOSITE BELOW: *The Allied landings had the benefit of very heavy naval fire support from a host of warships, small and large, the latter here represented by the British battleship* Rodney, *which carried nine 16-inch (406-mm) guns.*

Operation
Overlord

German defenses in depth. The Allies were ashore and from then on never looked like being driven off. The only major problem occurred at the front of the U.S. V Corps, where all but two of the DD tanks foundered in the rough sea and the infantry, checked by heavy fire, lay down on the beach, their morale entirely lost, until late afternoon. Then leadership began to assert itself, and the 1st Division was inland by nightfall.

By June 12 Montgomery had 326,000 men ashore and the series of battles necessary to put the second half of the plan into action had fairly begun. There was much misunderstanding of this plan, which was Montgomery's own, at the time, and some ill-informed criticism of alleged failure on the part of his troops. In fact, both Montgomery's army group of British, Poles and Canadians and Lieutenant-General Omar N. Bradley's Americans fought with great tenacity against the best professional soldiers of modern times, and broke them. In brief, the questioned strategy was for Montgomery's group to attack on the left, around Caen, where a break-out would spell the greatest danger to the Germans and where they would be expected to mass their reserves. This would ease Bradley's task in the west, where he was battering away at the defense perimeter hemming him in, in order to make a gap for his armored divisions under Patton to burst out into the open country and the enemy rear. In fact, this is what happened, and Montgomery reached the Seine 11 days

earlier than he had predicted in his plan.

Once the first phase of seizing and expanding the foothold in Normandy was over Montgomery, with overall operational control, commanded his own 21st Army Group (Canadian 1st and British 2nd Armies) and Bradley's 12th Army Group (U.S. 1st and 3rd

Armies). The last of these, under Lieutenant-General George S. Patton, had been formed in the field during the fighting. Bradley was promoted to 12th Army Group commander from the 1st Army, whose command was taken over by Lieutenant-General Courtney H. Hodges.

On July 7 Montgomery reduced Caen to rubble with heavy bombers, a fact which served only to block the line of advance of his own tanks, and then on July 18, in Operation Goodwood, tried to drive three armored divisions down an avenue 4,000 yards (3660m) wide, blasted open by more than 5,000 tons of bombs. Most of this tonnage hit nothing but the soil of France, for conforming to their usual tactics, the Germans' main defense line was several miles in the rear and this mighty hammer blow fell only on their outposts. The three armored divisions found themselves facing an unshaken defense. They lost rather more than half their tanks, mainly to the guns, but the 1st Panzer Division claimed 80 destroyed in counterattacks using their new Panther battle tanks. This was rough going, but the British and Canadians had by June 29 attracted four Panzer divisions to their sector. After a pause imposed by storms, which turned the whole Normandy battlefield into mud, Montgomery maintained the pressure on the left by repeated sledgehammer blows against the yielding, but still unbroken, fence of guns and tanks facing the 21st Army Group.

Then, on July 25, Bradley struck the decisive blow of the second phase, from St. Lô to the west, to capture Coutances in Operation Cobra. It was on the same pattern as Goodwood, with massive air support, but was larger and on a wider front. The air bombardment included 1,500 heavy and 400 medium bombers, but the main effort was made by infantry supported by tanks, with hundreds of fighter-bombers acting as close-support

ABOVE: *U.S. and British paratroopers get together in the latter part of the Normandy campaign.*

LEFT: *A French civilian couple and their friends hear the news of their liberation in company with their American liberators.*

OPPOSITE: *U.S. troops on board a landing craft. The ships which transported the assault divisions, and those which provided protection and fire support, probably constituted the greatest concentration of ships the world has ever seen.*

flying artillery. These were linked to the forward battalions by radio, using the new techniques for air–ground co-operation, and as soon as the tanks or infantry ran into opposition the aircraft were in action within a few minutes.

On August 1 Patton's 3rd Army was able to break through south of Coutances to begin the third phase of open warfare. He was able to clear enough of Brittany to remove any threat from the remaining German garrisons, then, on Bradley's orders on August 4, his axis swung from south-west to due east toward Paris. This was, perhaps, a strategic error, as it led to the failure of all attempts to trap the German 7th Army in the "Falaise pocket."

At this point, fortunately for the Allies, Hitler took charge. On July 29, when von Rundstedt advised him that the Battle of the Beach-head was lost and that the moment had arrived to retreat and establish a new defense line, running north and south along the Seine, Hitler dismissed the veteran but highly capable field-marshal. Rommel had been wounded, and the new commander was Field-Marshal Günther-Hans von Kluge, a good professional like all the German generals, but lacking the nerve necessary to stand up to Hitler.

Hitler saw a peculiar picture on his situation map. From the eastern end of the semi-circular bulge, marking the Allied perimeter, there appeared a long shoot moving first to the south and then veering to the east as it lengthened. This was the U.S. 3rd Army, and Hitler ordered von Kluge to advance into the loop and cut the tentacle off at its root at Avranches. Von Kluge dutifully assembled six divisions, including 250 tanks, all clearly visible to Allied air reconnaissance, and launched them, fatally, so that the head of the force was jammed between the expanding bridgehead and Patton's army. At this moment Montgomery ordered the Canadians to attack southward to Falaise and Patton to swing one of his corps north to meet it, so that the German counteroffensive was now threatened in its rear. Von Kluge requested but was denied permission to withdraw, and was ordered to advance to Avranches. The

German 7th Army was now crammed into a narrow corridor 40 miles (65km) long, its tanks and vehicles blocking the roads three abreast to present a target for the air forces, which massacred them. Meanwhile, the Canadians and Poles were fighting their way toward Falaise and Patton's XV Corps had captured Argentan, 15 miles (24km) away.

Fighting as German soldiers always did, the 2nd Panzer Division, against heavy odds and bombarded from the air, threw back the Canadians and held the gap open just long enough to enable some thousands of men to escape the trap, but the bulk of 15 divisions and 2,000 tanks and vehicles were destroyed.

WORLD WAR II

Chapter Five
THE INVASION OF SOUTHERN FRANCE
AND THE ALLIES PUSH ON TO THE SIEGFRIED LINE

The second French front was to be opened on the coast of the country in Operation Dragoon. At the strategic level the concept was valid: by mid-August, which was the earliest time the operation could be launched, the German last-ditch **garrisons** still held the Atlantic ports in western France and the Allies' two northern army groups were still being maintained across the Normandy beaches, so that the Allies' **logistical** situation would be eased if Toulon and Marseille could be taken intact, and divisions waiting in the USA could be ferried over to join in the fight; the quickest way to end the war was to destroy the armies defending Germany's western frontier, so this was the point at which the maximum force would be concentrated. Ideally, Dragoon should have been launched at the same time as Overlord, but there were not enough landing and other craft. It was not until August 15 that three divisions of Lieutenant-General Alexander M. Patch's U.S. 7th Army assaulted the stretch of coast extending from the east of Toulon to St. Raphaël. On the next day, the leading divisions of the French 1st Army, commanded by General Jean Marie Gabriel de Lattre de Tassigny, landed near St. Tropez, their mission being to capture and clear the two ports. De Lattre's initial status was as a corps commander under Patch, but, once his mission had been achieved, he would separate to lead his army as its full complement came ashore, his French 1st and the U.S. 7th Armies forming the 6th Army Group under Lieutenant-General Jacob L. Devers. The 6th Army Group's axis was to be north toward Grenoble and Belfort, and then east to arrive on the right of Lieutenant-General Bradley's 12th Army Group.

Words to Understand

Garrison: A military installation where troops are stationed.

Logistical: Relating to logistics.

Pillbox: A concrete emplacement for machine guns and antitank weapons.

The opposition faced by Dragoon was numerically formidable, consisting as it did of Colonel-General Johannes von Blaskowitz's Army Group G with 11 divisions. These divisions, however, were of poor quality and, being mainly occupied in operations against the French Forces of the Interior (FFI, or "resistance"), were able to provide only a cordon defense of possible invasion beaches, which were therefore penetrated with ease. The Oberkommando der Wehrmacht (OKW, or armed forces high command) sensibly

opted to cut its losses and pull back. Von Blaskowitz was ordered to leave strong garrisons in Marseille and Toulon, in order to deny them to the Allies for as long as possible, and to withdraw his main strength up the valley of the Rhône river to the north, thus concentrating the remaining German forces for the defense of the Reich.

Dragoon was a text-book success. Some 400 aircraft dropped a composite U.S.-British airborne division to control the road network by which any counterattack forces might reach the beach-head. This was to be established by the U.S. 3rd, 45th and 1st Divisions, supported by the 36th Division and the 1st Combat Command of the French 1st Armored Division, all covered by a powerful air force and preceded by a tremendous naval bombardment. Patch immediately launched his VI Corps on two axes to hurry the German rearguards along, the left through Avignon and up the Rhône valley, and the right along the Route Napoléon through Digne and Grenoble.

De Lattre had been ordered to wait until his forces had been fully delivered, on about D+10, and then take Toulon. This looked like being a costly affair. The port was held by some 25,000 troops, ensconced in a ring of 30 forts of old vintage but proof against all but the heaviest weapons, and more modern defenses based on earthworks and **pillboxes**. A deliberate assault with maximum force was required, but to give a German commander ten days in which to improve his defenses still further seemed unwise. The initial landing had gone so smoothly and the turnaround of the ships had been so

OPPOSITE: U.S. airborne infantry of the Allied provisional airborne division prepare for their commitment in Operation Dragoon as they wait to board their Waco CG-4 Hadrian assault glider.

RIGHT: As the Allies landed and moved inland, members of the French resistance came to their aid, as indicated here, at Hyères, on the south coast of France just to the east of Toulon.

rapid, however, that the buildup was much faster than expected. De Lattre, therefore, opted not to wait and obtained the permission of Patch and Devers to begin his operation on August 20, five days ahead of schedule. De Lattre had the as yet incomplete 1st Free French Division (Brigadier-General Diégo Charles Joseph Brosset), 3rd Algerian Division (Major-General Joseph Jean Goislard de Monsabert), 9th

Colonial Division (Major-General Joseph Abraham Auguste Pierre Édouard Magnan) and 1st Free French Armoured Division (Major-General Jean Louis Alai Touzet du Vigier). The commanders were good and the French colonial infantry was adept at operating in broken country. There is a range of inland hills parallel with the coast, north of Hyères, all the way to Marseille, and this offered the most difficult, the most

unlikely, and therefore the most promising approach. Accordingly de Lattre sent Goislard de Monsabert, reinforced by a tabor (squadron) of *goumiers*, in a wide sweeping movement around the north and west of Toulon. The *goumiers* were the lethal, semi-regular Moroccan infantry enlisted by the French, who were allowed to wear their own dress and fight in their own way, specializing in reconnaissance and infiltration. Touzet du Vigier, still lacking one combat command, was launched on an even wider encircling movement outside Goislard de Monsabert to protect his right flank (no one knew, at this moment, the total extent of the German withdrawal) and to hook in south and west of Marseille. Patch had agreed to release his other combat command as soon as it could be disengaged, while Brosset, reinforced by French commandos, moved directly on the Hyères-Toulon axis. The 9th Division would be attached between the 3rd and the Free French as it disembarked, its units marching into action without pause.

The speed with which de Lattre developed his maneuver was astonishing. The German units may have been of

doubtful quality, but the Free French had to do some hard fighting for Hyères. Three strong forts, located on commanding heights outside Toulon, were taken only at the cost of severe casualties by the divisional reconnaissance regiment and the commandos, on August 22. In one of the forts, 250 German dead were counted. The reconnaissance regiment then slipped through the ring of pillboxes and strongpoints into the city center. Magnan went forward to see where to introduce his leading troops, returning to spur them on. An intensely confused situation then began to develop inside the city, with the badly shaken Germans holding on while Magnan's men surrounded them. Magnan was given the task of mopping up the port and, on August 26, the last strongholds surrendered and Toulon was free.

Encouraged by this success and guessing that the two things he must avoid were to check the élan of his troops or to give the Germans time, de Lattre decided to attack Marseille immediately, without waiting to consolidate. He disengaged Brosset, sending him together with the 1st Armored Division's Combat 1st Command (Brigadier-General Aimé Sudre) to join

de Monsabert, reinforcing him with more *goumiers* as they arrived. He then ordered the commanders to close in on a given line surrounding the city, without commiting themselves except to reconnaissance, until he could assess the situation on August 23. Marseille was defended by German marines, the 244th Infantry Division and a jumble of units, which had been scattered from the beach-head area by the shock of the U.S. VI Corps landing, and 200 assorted guns. To evict such a German garrison from a city in house-to-house fighting might have taken weeks in the old days, but with the whole population of the city against them and every street or suburban road on the perimeter offering a route for infiltration, and with scores of FFI squads harassing them, the German position was untenable. Nevertheless, de Lattre de Tassigny sensibly paused to regroup. He had, apart from his task of reducing Marseille, to cover the left flank of the U.S. VI Corps and as an army commander had to be thinking even further ahead and preparing his formations for the pursuit north. For this he had to assemble his 1st Armoured Division, less the tanks for the attack on Marseille.

All this was well-planned and the French staff work appears to have been both prompt and accurate. As it turned out, but happily enough, the forward troops did not take the slightest notice. Supported by the FFI, one combat team of Sudre's tanks and motorized infantry,

LEFT: *German prisoners being escorted to the rear along a road in southern France.*

OPPOSITE ABOVE: *The Allies had built up a good overall picture of the Siegfried Line right from the start of the war, when reconnaissance flights were flown by aircraft such as the Bristol Blenheim Mk IV twin-engined warplane.*

OPPOSITE BELOW: *U.S. infantrymen take a closer look at an undamaged part of the antitank defenses of the German Westwall or "Seigfried" Line, after the fighting had moved farther to the east.*

plus a battalion of de Monsabert's Algerians, penetrated into the heart of the city and began to wreak havoc. In a short time they were up against the inner defenses of the dock area, the ultimate objective of the whole operation. On the outside, the remainder of the 3rd Division, with two more tabors of *goumiers,* was steadily reducing the concrete defenses outside the city. Fortunately, the fortresses were stronger than the defenders, although the Algerians and the *goumiers,* without the benefit of prolonged or heavy bombardment, suffered severe casualties in clearing them. At the earliest possible moment, de Monsabert established his headquarters in the city. From here, he was able to establish contact with the German garrison commander, and after the French had carried the main defenses covering the docks, persuade him to surrender on August 27. Marseille thus fell one month ahead of schedule.

THE ALLIES PUSH ON TO THE SIEGFRIED LINE

By the first day of September 1944, Germany's defensive system on the "Western Front" had been destroyed. The men who had survived the catastrophe at Falaise had been scattered, and had lost most of their remaining equipment in a vain attempt to hold the line of the Seine river, which the Allied armies had crossed with great dash. Hitler had dismissed von Kluge, who committed suicide, and had replaced him with his favourite "fireman," Field-Marshal Walther Model. The new commander-in-chief in the west could only rally what troops he had and seek to create the defense of the frontiers of the Reich. The Westwall, the so-called "Siegfried" Line, was unmanned, and many of its guns had been removed for use in the east. The western frontier of Germany, in fact, was wide open to any fast-moving assault. Why Eisenhower did not attempt it has since been the subject of debate. Whatever the verdict, the factors include the major stumbling block that the Allies had given no thought to what

they should do after breaking out of their Normandy lodgement. There was no overall scheme, and the unexpectedness of their pre-schedule success had taken all the Allied generals by surprise. All the armies swung east or north-east and advanced as best they could. On September 1 the Canadian 1st Army was driving up the Channel coast, in the process providing relief to the cities and towns of southern England by overrunning the launching sites for V-1 flying bombs; the British 2nd Army was racing for Brussels; the U.S. 1st Army was some 80 miles (130km) past Pans; and the U.S. 3rd Army was as far forward as Verdun. The U.S. 7th Army and the newly-formed French 1st Army had advanced some 200 miles (320km)

north from their landing sites on the French Riviera. This General Dwight D. Eisenhower believed to be a satisfactory situation as he assumed full control of all operations and relegated General Sir Bernard Montgomery to the more limited command of his own British/Canadian 21st Army Group. Eisenhower favored a broad-front advance so that all his divisions could exert their full force, their flanks secure as they spread across France.

The immediate difficulty he faced was that, partly as a result of winning the Battle of Normandy 11 days ahead of schedule, the necessary ports had not yet been captured and cleared. Therefore, the supplies necessary for the vast Allied armies had still to come via the one

surviving Mulberry harbor, over the beaches and then up the lines of communication by lorry, for the Allied bombing campaign, which had totally wrecked the French railway system and made it useless to the Germans, had also, of course, denied its use to the Allies. Eisenhower had to feed some 2.25 million troops, and provide fuel for

ABOVE: *British armor passes through Falaise on the southern side of the Normandy lodgement at the time of the Allied break-out in August 1944.*

OPPOSITE: *A Universal (or Bren gun) Carrier of a Canadian airborne unit at Falaise, in August 1944.*

almost 450,000 vehicles, of which some 5,000 were front-line tanks. As the lines of communications lengthened, the supply lorries themselves began to consume supplies at an increasing rate: thus Eisenhower had to decide either to halt units not needed for the immediate pursuit, so that the available supplies could be delivered to small, spearhead formations, or the whole advance slowed down. If the advance was slowed, the Germans would have time to consolidate the defense of the frontier before the pursuing forces could arrive. The answer was simple, but its implementation was fraught with difficulties.

Montgomery argued vehemently and with considerable reason that the northern route was strategically the most important and that all resources should be concentrated on it for a swift major advance. However, this would have meant halting the U.S. 1st and 3rd Armies, which was impossible for political reasons: Eisenhower could not check his U.S. armies and give a British general the honor of winning the war with Germany. Bradley and Patton saw Montgomery's plan as the means for the British general to keep himself in the limelight. Patton was determined to press on, giving Eisenhower the choice of either halting (or even recalling) him, or of keeping him supplied. Even a supreme commander could not override two such powerful subordinates, and the best he could do was to give the northern front priority.

While the armies were advancing and high command was being distracted by argument and the problem of supply, it completely forgot that the key to a resolution of the supply problem, especially in the northern sector, was the rapid capture of Antwerp as a working port. Montgomery was intent on an expedient to accelerate his advance, namely the use of the airborne formations lying idle in England, to clear the network of river obstacles ahead of him as far as the bridge at Arnhem, in an operation to take place in mid-September. In the meantime the German resistance began to strengthen.

The Allied armies had some enjoyable weeks of motoring through

France with an occasional skirmish, but were then brought abruptly to a halt. The Westwall was not a line of fortifications in the same sense as was the Maginot Line. The Germans were superb exponents of the concept of defence in depth: each position was covered by more behind, and backing these were more parties of troops ready to counterattack and drive out successful intruders. Into this the Americans had to batter a way, bit by bit, with heavy artillery, while in the Netherlands the 21st Army Group was being hampered by the maze of defended waterways. The Allies had lost the race to the frontiers and the German "Watch on the Rhine" had been established.

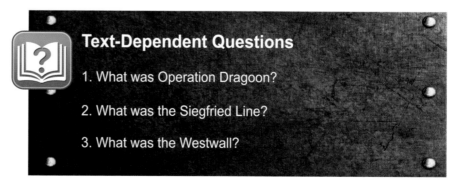

Text-Dependent Questions

1. What was Operation Dragoon?

2. What was the Siegfried Line?

3. What was the Westwall?

Research Projects

What part did the French Resistance play in aiding the success of the Allies in Western Europe in World War II?

WORLD WAR II

Chapter Six
THE BATTLES OF ARNHEM AND BULGE

Despite his rebuff by General Dwight D. Eisenhower, General Sir Bernard Montgomery was confident that the task of his 21st Army Group was the seizure of the Ruhr, Germany's industrial heartland, to which there were two avenues of approach. One extended due east, which would mean a bloody battle of attrition to breach the Westwall, and the other extended to the north-north-east, in the direction of Arnhem. The Westwall defenses ended near Cleve, and if Arnhem, with its great road bridge over the Rhine, could be secured, the defenses could be outflanked to the

north. This latter approach would not be easier than the former, for the Netherlands was the worst possible terrain for armored warfare, being flat, low-lying, wet, and divided by a network of dykes and drainage ditches. To reach the lower Rhine at Arnhem it was first necessary to cross three wide navigation canals as well as the Maas and Waal rivers. One option was as unattractive as the other for ground operations, but lying idle in England was the whole of Lieutenant-General Lewis H. Brereton's Allied 1st Airborne Army, inactive since D-Day. No fewer than 17 plans to

employ parts of this army had been made and canceled, generally because the objectives had been overrun by the ground forces, or because the weather had deteriorated and German resistance had stiffened.

Montgomery now revived and revised the original but unrealized "Comet" plan, for the seizure of Nijmegen and Arnhem by one reinforced division. This was now developed into the parallel "Market" airborne and 'Garden' land operations. The forward elements of the British 2nd Army had reached the Meuse-Escaut Canal, 70

miles (110km) from Arnhem, and crossed it south of Borkel. The new plan was to drop a whole airborne corps: the U.S. 101st Airborne Division, under Major-General James A. Gavin, would seize and hold the bridges over the Wilhelmina Canal at Son and the Willemswart at Veghel; the U.S. 82nd Airborne Division, under Major-General Maxwell D. Taylor, the bridges over the Maas at Grave and the Waal at Nijmegen; and the British 1st Airborne Division, under Major-General Roy Urquhart, the bridge at Arnhem in "Market." At the same time the British XXX Corps, under Lieutenant General B.G. Horrocks, would drive up the road through Eindhoven, which connected all these points, the Guards Armored Division leading, and join up, in "Garden," with the lightly-armed airborne troops as rapidly as possible. This armored advance was absolutely essential for success, as the strength of airborne forces lay in the surprise of their sudden descent, their weakness being a lack of heavy weapons, especially for prolonged defense against armor.

There were many who argued that the whole operation was too risky, but it was agreed by all responsible that it must go on. Planning had gone too far, the morale of the troops would be in danger if they were not used, and in any case the conduct of war is nothing but a choice between dangers. Great strategic rewards demand great tactical risks, and the tactical risks at Arnhem were clear enough. Airborne troops, most experts believed, should be dropped in the dark, to obtain the element of surprise, and as close to their objectives as possible, if not on top of them. For various reasons, of which the most telling was the belief of the Royal Air Force that the Arnhem area was strongly defended by

OPPOSITE: German troops at Arnhem, where ad hoc battle groups checked the British airborne soldiers for a time just long enough for heavier German units to reach the scene.

RIGHT: Captured British airborne soldiers with their Waffen-SS captors in the aftermath of the Arnhem fighting.

The Archer Antitank Gun

The success of Operations Market and Garden depended on the progress of the British XXX Corps from the Meuse-Escaut Canal to reach the British 1st Airborne Division before it succumbed to German counterattacks at Arnhem. There was only a single road, and the XXX Corps could advance at only a snail's pace in the face of German tank and artillery opposition. This is an Archer self-propelled antitank gun of the XXX Corps. The Archer was in essence the superb 17-pounder antitank gun on the hull of the obsolete Valentine infantry tank.

Color Footage of Operation Market Garden

antiaircraft artillery, the assault was made by day, the drop zones for the paratroops and the landing zone for the gliders being 8 miles (13km), or at least a three-hour march, from the vital bridge. Three hours is too much time to give gratuitously to an opponent, rightly feared for his ability to react rapidly and aggressively. Even so, if Urquhart had been able to implement his plan all might yet have turned out better: Urquhart proposed to put one whole brigade in close defense of the bridge and three more around it in a solid defense perimeter, giving him some 10,900 high-grade infantry supported by light artillery and 6-pounder antitank guns with which to hold off any counterattack. Unfortunately, the lack of aircraft imposed a three-day build-up over the period September 17–19, by which time only one battalion of the whole force had been able to reach its objective.

Another factor militating against Allied success was the date. The third week in September was too late, and this was not only on account of the weather. Intelligence showed that the efforts of Field-Marshal Walther Model, of Army Group B, to revitalize shattered German formations and man the Westwall were succeeding, and resistance was stiffening everywhere. The most serious problem was that the II SS Panzer Corps (9th and 10th SS Panzer Divisions), commanded by the able General Willi Bittrich, was in the Arnhem area to rest and re-equip: this fact was known to some Allied

intelligence agencies, but for a variety of reasons was ignored.

On the German side there had been much discussion about the next possible move by the Allies, but no firm plans had been made. But it had proved enough for Model to be in overall command in the area, with Colonel-General Kurt Student, himself a paratrooper, in command of the sector, and Bittrich in local command, with their headquarters in the vicinity of the drops. All acted immediately, and the speed of the three commanders was matched by that of the German soldiers, who were schooled to seize their weapons and throw themselves into action at once, without panic or even doubt, under the first leader who rallied them. German officers were expected to behave as the situation demanded without asking permission or waiting for orders. The II SS Panzer Corps was therefore immediately appropriated; Student called up some parachute Kampfgruppen (ad hoc battle groups) from the Köln area, and took control of an infantry division passing by train through his sector to another command. In a very short time the German defenses

were being mobilized and local counterattacks were being mounted.

A series of misfortunes was about to fall upon the luckless 1st Airborne Division, which no amount of heroism could overcome, the first of which was a stop line of youths of an SS Panzergrenadier training battalion. Behind this was another battle group from the 9th SS Panzer Division's infantry, with some light armored vehicles, with another forming and a third hastening to the road bridge. The airborne troops were therefore involved in precisely the kind of operation for which they were not fitted: an attack by light infantry on a strong all-arms force, without the benefit of armored cooperation and heavy artillery

ABOVE: *The sky fills with parachutes as the British 1st Airborne Division descends toward its drop zones outside, and in fact too far outside, Arnhem.*

OPPOSITE: *A 25-pounder field gun of the Canadian 5th Field Regiment in action near Nijmegen.*

firepower. All the same, Lieutenant-Colonel John Frost managed to fight his way with most of his 2nd Parachute Battalion to the Arnhem road bridge, and there held on.

The second misfortune was the German discovery, on the body of a U.S. officer killed in a glider crash, an operation order outlining the entire plan. Thus Student and Bittrich knew in a matter of hours every move to make: thus revealed, the LZs near Arnhem were soon ringed by AA guns. The third misfortune was the complete failure of the 1st Airborne Division's radio sets, with the sole exception of the light regiment of the Royal Artillery. Thus

everyone from Urquhart's headquarters, down to battalions, was out of touch with one another and the air force. Urquhart himself went forward with one brigadier but was unable even to talk back from his own jeep to his own headquarters, only 2 miles (3.2km) distant, and was himself caught up in the fighting and was unable to get back, while the brigadier was wounded. The command system thus disintegrated at this crucial stage of the battle, and the battle itself into a series of bitter but wholly uncoordinated small combats. Only Frost's battalion, less one company but with some divisional troops who had rallied to him, hung on grimly to the area

commanding the north end of the unblown Arnhem road bridge. The rail bridge had been blown in the face of Frost's C Company, which had been ordered to take it.

Meanwhile things had been going successfully, if behind schedule, on the road from the south. The Americans had had a much easier landing, so their troubles started only later, when Student's counterattacks began. By September 18 the 101st Division had a firm grip on their objectives and had linked with the tank battalion of the Irish Guards. Eindhoven was clear, while farther to the north, the 82nd Airborne Division had the bridge over the Maas at Grave and

was fighting hard in Nijmegen for access to the Waal bridge. The Guards Armoured Division's tanks, supported by the guns of the XXX Corps and air attacks, were rolling, but soon came to a halt. It was impossible to deploy off the roads without bogging down, and to make matters worse the roads ran along high embankments, along which the tanks were perfect targets, silhouetted against the sky, for the 3.465-inch (88-mm) antitank guns sited on both sides. Making matters worse, the weather worsened, so that both the air resupply of the men at Arnhem and the provision of air support to the troops fighting up the road were interrupted. Thus it was not until September 22 that a great combined effort pushed elements of the British 43rd and U.S. 82nd Divisions across the Waal

and secured the Nijmegen bridge. But on the same day the Guards Armored Division had to send a brigade back to assist the 101st Division at Veghel, where it was being attacked from the east and west simultaneously. Although the fighting along the corridor was severe, it was overshadowed by the tragedy in Arnhem: the 82nd Division lost 1,400 men and the 101st Division more than 2,000; they were to lose another 3,600 between them before the ground taken was finally secured.

In Arnhem close-quarter fighting of savage intensity continued unabated. By September 19 Urquhart appreciated that he was not able to fight his way through to reinforce Frost or take up his planned positions, and decided to form a close defensive perimeter in the small town of

BELOW: Survivors by the wreckage of their Waco CG-4 Hadrian glider. It was the task of the U.S. 101st Airborne Division to take and hold the bridges over the Wilhelmina Canal at Zon and the Zuit Willemsvaart Canal at Veghel.

OPPOSITE ABOVE: British airborne troops load the trailer of their Jeep from an Airspeed Horsa assault glider outside Arnhem. By comparison with the German formations in the area, the British troops lacked heavy weapons but fought with great courage and determination to hold their positions for considerably longer than had been thought possible.

OPPOSITE BELOW: A British 6-pounder anti-tank gun in action at Arnhem. This was the heaviest antitank weapon which the Allies could deliver by air.

Osterbeek on the northern bank of the Rhine, 4 miles (6.5km) downstream of Arnhem. If he and Frost, at the northern end of the Arnhem bridge, could hold out in house-to-house fighting there was still a chance that the XXX Corps might break through in time, but this hope soon faded. The division nonetheless fought on. After tragic delay, the Polish 1st Independent Parachute Brigade Group was dropped opposite Osterbeek, south of the river, but its task was impossible: the brigade suffered heavy casualties on landing, and could neither cross the river to reinforce Urquhart nor turn south to help open the road, for Bittrich had sent a battalion of Panzergrenadiers with a company of Panther tanks to block it.

The situation at the end of the week was that the 9th SS Panzer Division was

systematically reducing the Arnhem positions, while the 10th SS Panzer Division was still blocking the last few miles between the XXX Corps and the Arnhem bridge, and both the U.S. airborne divisions were under counterattack from east and west. It soon became clear that the only course was to use the infantry of the British 43rd Division to close up to the river bank at Osterbeek and evacuate what was left of Urquhart's formation before they were killed or captured. The division achieved its task with courage and skill, actually making an assault crossing to the north

bank, while the massed guns of the XXX Corps put a box barrage around Osterbeek, and the engineers in boats brought out most of the unwounded men of the garrison under intense fire. So intense was the whole level of the fighting and so numerous the acts of gallantry that this fine feat was not seen as very remarkable. Some idea of the nature of the fighting is discernible from the casualty figures: the 1st Airborne Division lost 6,400 men, of whom 1,200 were killed, while the 9th SS Panzer Division and its reinforcing units lost 3,500 men.

ABOVE: *The bridge over the Nederrijn (lower Rhine) at Arnhem. The British managed to take and hold the northern end until eventually forced to surrender, but the Germans held the southern end throughout the battle.*

OPPOSITE: *Paratroopers of the U.S. 101st Airborne Division at Bastogne, where they fought as conventional infantry against the encircling Germans in the Battle of the Bulge. Here they recover parachuted supplies.*

THE "BATTLE OF THE BULGE"

On December 15, 1944 three German armies crashed into a weakly-held sector of the Allied front in a hopeless counteroffensive, known to the Germans at the time as *Wacht am Rhein* (Watch on the Rhine) and later to the world at large as the "Battle of the Bulge." By January 28, 1945 the Germans were back on their start lines, leaving behind 19,000 dead as well as 111,000 wounded, missing or taken prisoner, and having lost hundreds of irreplaceable tanks and assault guns. In the matter of timing Hitler's intuition, always better than his strategy, had been perfect. By the end of the year the Allies were mentally balanced between the over-confidence born of their great victories and the unpleasant shock, particularly to the Americans, of what was involved in trying to break into the Westwall. This involved a series of costly battles, reminiscent of the static meatgrinding of World War I. But breaching the Westwall was only a matter of time and resources: the long term assessment was that the German war machine was running down, and that lack of fuel for its armor would prevent anything but a dogged defense for what remained of the war. Some intelligence staffs had noticed some significant troop movements and predicted, correctly, the fact but not the location of an offensive. No notice was taken, and there was an air of cautious relaxation along all the U.S. and, to a lesser extent, British sectors of the front, except those opposite the Westwall.

Hitler planned to repeat the success of 1940 with a Blitzkrieg offensive through the least likely and therefore most weakly-held part of the Allied front, namely the Ardennes region and its forests, hills, steep ridges and deep ravines. Three armies, under the command of Field-Marshal Walther Model's Army Group B, were to take part: the newly-created 6th Panzerarmee of Colonel-General "Sepp" Dietrich was to make for Liège and Antwerp; the 5th Panzerarmee, under General Hasso-Eccard von Manteuffel, was to head for the vital communication center at Bastogne, and from there to Namur and Brussels, and thence Antwerp; and the 7th Army, under General Erich

Brandenburger, was to break through and swing left to protect von Manteuffel's left from a counterattack from the south. The German buildup was undertaken in the utmost secrecy, and it was a week before the Allied commanders discovered the Germans' intentions: at first they imagined it to be merely a spoiling attack to hinder the advance of Lieutenant-General Patton's U.S. 3rd Army toward the Saar.

Fortunately for the Allies, the Germans no longer had the resources for war on this scale, or the men, tanks, aircraft, or even fuel. The bulk of the new Volksgrenadier (people's grenadier) infantry comprised under-age boys and old men, who fought with courage and determination but without the battle craft of their predecessors. Even the once-elite paratroops, of whom two divisions were used, were of a low standard. Only the tank crews of the superb PzKpfw V Panther battle and PzKpfw VI Tiger heavy tanks were up to the old standard, and many of the junior officers and sergeants, bred in the old German tradition, were full of the attacking spirit.

The Allied high command was nonetheless taken completely by surprise when there began an offensive by nine Panzer and Panzergrenadier divisions, as well as 12 infantry divisions, totaling some 700 tanks and supported by 2,000 field guns. These forces smashed into and through a thin screen of only nine U.S. infantry regiments, backed by one armored division spread out over 100 miles (160km) of front in little more than an outpost line with no main line of resistance behind it. The troops themselves were either resting, like the 4th Division, severely handled in recent Westwall fighting, or new to the theater and only half-trained, like the 106th Division fresh from the USA. The U.S. situation was worsened by very severe weather, low morale, and the fact that much equipment (especially radio sets) were being serviced or repaired. The VII and VIII Corps of Lieutenant-General Courtney H. Hodges's US 1st Army in this sector were totally unprepared, morally and physically, to receive a massive offensive.

Early in the morning of December 16 the U.S. forward posts came under a

seasoned and green, fought hard and well. It is the response to initial defeat, with communications cut and total confusion abroad, which is the acid test of any army, and this the U.S. forces passed with distinction.

Counterattacking where they could and grimly hanging on where they could not, the U.S. soldiers held points vital in the terrain, such as crossroads, bridges, and communication centers, and offering little opportunity for cross-country tank maneuver. St. Vith and Houffalize held out for long enough and Bastogne, where six roads meet, did not fall. These and a host of other brave actions checked the Germans, as a result of which the entire schedule for *Wacht am Rhein* was delayed, buying the time for the resources of Lieutenant-General Omar N. Bradley's U.S. 12th Army Group to be redirected and positioned for a massive counterstroke. All the same, the picture as seen from the headquarters of

violent bombardment in the dark and prevailing fog, followed by a major assault. Almost inevitably there was a measure of panic in the American ranks, the front was broken in many places, some troops fled to the rear, artillery were abandoned, and many men surrendered. Most men, however, both

numerous Allied formations was enough to cause great dismay. Accurate information was at a premium and not readily available, so no one knew how well the fragments of the 1st Army were still fighting. What seemed ominous was that the front had been shattered, and particularly mortifying was the fact that U.S. soldiers were being actually outfought and, worse, surrendering in droves. The 28th Division was effectively destroyed, and the 106th Division had lost its two forward regiments, which were encircled and corralled inside a thin German cordon. All the rear areas, rich in food, munitions, and petrol stocks, seemed wide open to capture.

From the first day of *Wacht am Rhein*, the winter weather had included snow, low cloud, and fog, and this had grounded the most devastating Allied weapon, its tactical air power. Command decisions were difficult as the German salient, driven into the Ardennes, separated Hodges and most of his 1st Army from Bradley's 12th Army Group headquarters and Patton's US 3rd Army in the south.

General Dwight D. Eisenhower, the allied supreme commander, saw the correct solution at once and insisted on it to Bradley and Patton. Eisenhower placed the U.S. armies north of the bulge, the 1st and 9th under the command of Field-Marshal Montgomery, with instructions to hold the line of the Meuse, to shorten the defence line by withdrawing if it

OPPOSITE ABOVE: German troops with U.S. prisoners in the Ardennes.

OPPOSITE BELOW: The few U.S. divisions holding the front in the first stage of the Battle of the Bulge were green formations gaining acclimatization, or experienced formations sent to a quiet sector to rest and recuperate after a long time spent in combat.

ABOVE: A German Tiger II tank passes a column of U.S. prisoners taken during the Ardennes offensive.

became necessary, to create a reserve, and then to attack from the north. The 3rd Army was to cease its battle of attrition along the Saar, and swing north to make a massive blow against the German southern flank. Nothing was more to Patton's taste, and the feat performed by his staff of picking up the bulk of his army, turning it through a right angle to start it marching north across the cluttered lines of communication was exemplary. The only snag arose from bad Anglo-U.S. relations and a difference in outlook. Bradley, in particular, was incensed that any U.S. troops should be placed under British command, especially when that commander was Montgomery. The U.S. Army, furthermore, did not believe in withdrawal, even for the best tactical reasons. Thus Bradley privately ordered Hodges to ignore the orders to withdraw and go over to the attack as soon as possible.

Montgomery's highly professional moves secured the line of the Meuse using his own troops, thus freeing Hodges and Lieutenant-General William H. Simpson to organize the northern

counteroffensive with their U.S. 1st and 9th Armies. At the western tip of the German advance, the Panzer-Lehr and 2nd Panzer Divisions met the U.S. 2nd Armored Division and the British 3rd Royal Tank Regiment, the only British unit to be seriously engaged, near Dinant, while Patton's three corps attacked north-east, astride the Bastogne axis and into the base of the salient due north of Luxembourg. Patton's tactics, based on an unprepared headlong rush, proved very costly against unbroken Panzer units, but success was worth the cost. The turning point in the battle was in fact a change in the weather: the cold increased, with mud and slush turned to hard-frozen ground, the clouds and fog lifting to allow the sun to shine through. This was ideal flying weather, and the U.S. 9th Army Air Force flew 10,305 sorties in the period December 23–31. Thus the fate of Army Group B was sealed. The cost to the Americans was men and matériel they could replace, but as far as the Germans were concerned, their losses in the offensive were absolute, thus opening the door of the Third Reich to the Allies.

WORLD WAR II

Chapter Seven

THE BOMBER OFFENSIVE 1943–1945
AND THE END OF THE ROAD FOR NAZI GERMANY

At the Casablanca Conference of January 1943, Prime minister Winston Churchill and President Franklin D. Roosevelt met at Casablanca to decide on the general strategy of the war after the Axis forces had been expelled from Africa. High on the list of matters to be decided was the manner in which the efforts of the Royal Air Force's Bomber Command and the U.S. 8th Army Air Force, both based in the UK, could be coordinated to devastate the war-making capability of the Axis powers. Bomber production was still increasing, so in the months to come the force would continue to develop still further as a devastating weapon. Now Churchill and Roosevelt, together with their military advisers, had to select and prioritize the types of target to be attacked. The result was the "Pointblank" directive, which laid down the types of target to be attacked. The prioritization of the targets was later changed with considerable frequency, but was initially U-boat construction yards, aircraft manufacturing, transportation systems, oil plants, and other targets vital to the German armaments industry. The British were allowed to continue their night raids on centers of civilian population.

While the implications of the directive were assessed and revised target lists created, the bombing effort continued as before. By the middle of the year, however, a new sense of purpose was discernible in the activities of Bomber Command and the 8th AAF, joined from October 1943 onwards by the U.S. 9th AAF, operating from bases in the Foggia area of southern Italy. In the period June 20–24, Bomber Command undertook its first "shuttle" mission, in which aircraft setting off from the UK bombed

Words to Understand

Armaments: Military weapons that are used to fight a war.

Ballistic: Relating to ballistics or the motion of projectiles in flight.

Baltic: Relating to the Baltic Sea.

Wilhelmshaven, then flew on to North Africa, the Italian naval base of La Spezia being attacked on the return trip. Nine days earlier the 8th AAF had attacked the U-boat yards at Wilhelmshaven, but caused only slight damage. The problem currently hampering the 8th AAF was the lack of escort fighters with adequate range to escort the bombers to and from their targets, and it was not until the end of the year that the North American P-51 Mustang arrived, allowing the bombers to make deep penetration raids with proper escort all the way. The Americans devoted July to attacks on the German aircraft industry, principally the part producing fighters. Although the short-term results were good, the concentrated raids finally made the Germans see the wisdom of dispersing their production facilities, and this was now set in hand as a matter of urgency. At the end of July the British struck the first major blow against a German city, when massive raids destroyed nearly all of Hamburg, the firestorms caused by the incendiaries being responsible for most of the damage. Apart from their dead, the Germans had also been left with about 750,000 homeless, and this seriously impeded the effort to restore the city to a functioning level after the raids. On the

night of August 17–18 Bomber Command then struck at the German secret weapon research center at Peenemünde on Germany's Baltic coast. Although not absolutely certain of the importance of the target, Bomber Command effected a heavy raid, which caused much damage, slowing down the development of the V-2 ballistic missile.

The Americans now learned a hard lesson on the need for escort fighters on deep penetration missions. On August 1 178 bombers set off from North Africa to bomb the oilfields at Ploesti in Romania. Picked up by German radar in Greece, the bomber force was harried mercilessly by German and Romanian fighters, losing 54 of its number. Damage was caused to the refinery, but did not halt production for long, and as if this were not enough, the Americans next lost 60 out of 376 bombers dispatched to strike the ball-bearing factories at Schweinfurt. A similar raid on October 14 was even more costly, with 60 bombers lost out of 291. The machine guns of the bombers were not enough to defeat the cannon-armed fighters, flown by the Germans with great determination and courage. After the Schweinfurt debacle, the Americans suspended deep-penetration daylight missions pending the arrival of P-51 escort fighters. The first of these arrived on December 3, and the Americans then resumed their daylight offensive.

The culmination of the British bombing year was the beginning of the Battle of Berlin in November. Up to March 1944, some 16 major raids had been targeted against the German capital, causing great damage and giving the Germans a very hard time of it. By this time the British bomber force had been joined by large numbers of the latest bomber, the comparatively small de Havilland Mosquito. Of wooden construction and powered by two engines, the Mosquito was able to carry a very useful bomb load, and was in fact a far more cost-effective aircraft than most heavy bombers. It could deliver its bomb load with great accuracy at all altitudes, although its optimum was low to medium altitude, and its speed made it more than a match for any German fighter. So versatile was the basic design that all sorts of variants of the aircraft were produced: night-fighter, attack-fighter, fighter-bomber, passenger transport, photographic reconnaissance platform and meteorological workhorse. The German night-fighters were also improving, and the electronic battle became very intense late in 1943 and early in 1944. By this time, the British were also using a number of electronic navigational aids, with good results.

During the first half of 1944, relentless pressure was maintained against Germany. The Americans had now grouped together as the Strategic Air Forces, under Lieutenant-General Carl A. Spaatz, the 8th AAF in England and the 15th AAF in Italy enabling a single command organization to direct very large numbers of bombers onto the chosen targets with great ease. Spaatz also worked closely with Air Chief-Marshal Sir Arthur Harris in co-ordinating the U.S. and British efforts: a target might well be visited by Bomber Command in the night and by the 8th and/or 15th AAFs on the following day, or vice versa.

Most important for the Americans, however, was the "Big Week" effort during the period February 20–26, 1944,

the object of which was to grind down German fighter strength. Although Bomber Command raided the same targets at night, the week was essentially a U.S. effort. While the bombers attacked fighter manufacturing factories to destroy the Germans' source of supply, the escort fighters had a field day with the German fighters sent aloft to attack the bombers. Here the true worth of the superb Mustang was shown to its full extent. Although Spaatz lost 244 bombers and 33 fighters during the Big Week, the Germans lost 692 fighters in the air, plus many more on the ground and in the factories. The factories themselves were also severely damaged. The same basic task of grinding down the Luftwaffe was continued through to May, causing the Germans to lose 2,442 fighters in action and 1,500 more from other causes.

There was now a change in the emphasis of the bombing campaign. The strategic bombers were relieved of conventional targets and were tasked with the isolation of the forthcoming battlefield in northern France. The object of this campaign of May and June 1944 was the preparation of the

area for the Allied landings in Normandy. Both the strategic and tactical air forces were employed to destroy all the means of communication in northern France, the Low Countries and western Germany. Tunnels were caved in, bridges dropped, railway lines cut, marshaling yards destroyed, canals breached, and roads bombed. The idea behind the campaign was that Normandy and Brittany be isolated, so that in June, when the Allies landed, the Germans would be unable to rush up reinforcements with their usual speed. Great care had to be taken, however, that no pattern emerged from the bombing lest the Germans deduced where the landings were to take place. At the same time as this campaign was being waged, the Allied air forces were attacking and ruining nearly every airfield in the area. By the time of the Normandy landings, there were scarcely any German aircraft in northern France,

ABOVE: There being no defense against the V-2 ballistic missiles in flight, the Allies sought to destroy them during their manufacture.

The B17 Flying Fortress

One of the two mainstays of the U.S. heavy bomber effort in the European theater was the Boeing B-17 Flying Fortress, seen here in its ultimate B-17G form, with a chin barbette carrying two 0.5-inch (12.7-mm) machine guns to deter head-on attacks by German fighters.

and those which had survived the Allied onslaught had been withdrawn.

Once the Allied landings had secured the intended initial lodgement, the strategic bombers returned to their task of destroying Germany's ability and will to wage war. From July to December the heavy bomber campaign reached its peak. Virtually without a break, British and U.S. bombers concentrated their attacks on the Germany transport system, oil industry, and other sources of power. By the end of 1944, Germany's ability to fight a war had at last been seriously affected. There was little fuel left for vehicles and aircraft, and even though the production of matériel was still rising, the Germans had no way of delivering such guns, tanks, and aircraft to the fighting troops. And even if the troops had received them, they could not run them. To all intents and purposes, by the end of 1944 Germany had been paralyzed by her lack of fuel and the absence of a transport system.

The strategic bombing campaign continued into 1945, with German resistance slowly dying away. Even though the Germans had the best turbojet-powered fighter of the war, the Messerschmitt Me 262, which could have posed a very real threat to Allied air superiority in 1944, the type had not been placed in full-scale production early enough, and the few examples in operation were unable to stem the tide. With no fuel for training, the German

pilots had also deteriorated in quality from the great days of 1940 to 1943.

The area bombing concept reached its conclusion on the night of February 13–14, when the baroque city of Dresden was utterly destroyed. Although the city had little military significance, and was full of refugees fleeing from the Soviets, a great Bomber Command raid was launched. The incendiaries took an immediate hold in the old city, and uncontrollable firestorms of horrific intensity swept all before them. The 8th AAF completed Bomber Command's work with a great raid on the day after the RAF's night attack.

The last remnants of the Luftwaffe were eliminated in the period March 21–24, when the Allies' air forces flew more than 40,000 missions to seek out these last survivors of the German air force. Thereafter, the strategic bomber force was used in direct support of the ground forces for the rest of the war.

THE END OF THE ROAD FOR NAZI GERMANY

In 1944 the Soviet forces on the Eastern Front had launched three major offensives, all of which succeeded: the spring offensive had pushed the Germans back out of the Ukraine and away from Leningrad; the summer offensive had concentrated in the central sector of the front, and had driven the Axis forces out of Belorussia, back into Poland and the Baltic states, and had halted with its spearheads just outside Warsaw; the autumn offensive had once again been a two-part drive, the Ukrainian fronts having been pushed back in the south and the Axis forces back into the Balkans, before being forced to retreat into Hungary and Czechoslovakia after the defections of Bulgaria and Romania; in the north, the Baltic fronts had moved

OPPOSITE LEFT: *The ruins of the German city of Dresden after the combined British and U.S. attacks on it in February 1945.*

OPPOSITE RIGHT: *Bearing the weight of the British night-bombing offensive by Germany was the Avro Lancaster heavy bomber and its seven-man crew.*

forward once again, driving through to the Baltic and trapping Army Group North in the Kurland peninsula.

The Soviets were now poised near to the borders of Germany, the curtain for the final act rising on January 12, 1945 when the armies of Marshal K.K. Rokossovsky's 2nd Belorussian Front swept over the Narew river just north of Warsaw and fell on the German 2nd Army. At the same time, the Soviet 47th Army set about taking Warsaw, which fell 17 January 17. Rokossovsky's troops drove all before them, advancing north-west up the right bank of the Vistula river toward the Baltic, and cutting off Colonel-General Georg-Hans Reinhardt's Army Group Center near the sea between Elbing and Danzig.

While its right was being threatened by Rokossovsky's front, Army Group Center also found its left to be in no better position: General I.D. Chernyakovsky's 3rd Belorussian Front had also driven forward, in conjunction with General I. K. Bagramyan's 1st Baltic Front, to reach the sea north of Memel. Reinhardt had begged to be allowed to disperse his forces in order to meet this threat, but Hitler had refused, and now the whole army group had been cut off and was in desperate straits. By February 8 500,000 Germans had been pinned

against the coast in a few isolated pockets. Hitler at last saw that he had been wrong and gave permission for the survivors to be taken off. This the German navy did, in an extraordinary evacuation quite the equal of Dunkirk, leaving the last German beach-heads to hold out as best they could for the rest of the war, the last surrendering only on May 9. Some of the troops in Kurland were pulled out at the same time, as were some 1.5 million civilians. But the cost was appalling, as the Germans had no air cover to fight off the Soviet attack warplanes: by the end of the evacuation the German navy comprised only one heavy and one light cruiser.

Having fallen, East Prussia was the first part of the Third Reich to be taken by the USSR in World War II.

While these northern forces were taking East Prussia, the armies of Marshal Georgi Zhukov's 1st Belorussian Front and Marshal I.S. Konev's 1st Ukrainian Front had been surging forward under devastating artillery support across the Vistula river to the south of Warsaw. Only the 9th, 4th Panzer, and 17th Armies of Colonel-General Johannes Harpe's Army Group A were there to make the vain effort to stop the Soviets. The German task was impossible, and by January 17 the Soviets had advanced almost to the German-Polish border near Katowice and Czestochowa. Confident of their vastly superior manpower and matériel strength, Zhukov and Konev pressed on as far and as fast as their logistics organizations could support them. These organizations had a difficult task: more than 1.5 million Soviet soldiers were pressing steadily forward, supported by 28,000 guns, nearly 3,500 tanks and self-propelled guns and some 10,000 aircraft. The Germans, on the other hand, could not find even a fraction of the supplies needed by their 600,000 men, 8,250 guns, 700 tanks and 1,300 aircraft, despite the fact that they were working on interior lines of communication.

Zhukov, in particular, appeared to be moving forward irresistibly, and by January 31 the 1st Belorussian Front reached the Oder river, only some 40 miles (65km) east of Berlin. In Zhukov's rear, however, as in everyone else's, there were large numbers of German pockets, bypassed and contained in the furious advance, but now ready to be mopped up. Most of the smaller pockets were eliminated in short order, but some held out for long periods in dogged displays of defensive fighting. As ever insistent on the need to hold ground, Hitler had demanded that key cities, such as Deutsche Krone, Poznan, Glogau, Breslau, and Oppeln be held, and held they were for some time, in some cases right up to the end of the war.

Zhukov's great central drive had also had the effect of splitting Army Groups A and Vistula, the latter surprisingly commanded by Reichsführer-SS Heinrich Himmler, who had apparently decided he was as capable as the next man of leading an army group, without any military training. Admittedly his force was nothing but a motley of troops, but this was all the more reason to have had an experienced commander. After a short time Himmler retired from his command in favor of Colonel-General Gotthard Heinrici, who was able to pull the command together to a certain extent.

In the middle of February both Soviet fronts attacked again, Zhukov's in Pomerania and Konev's in Silesia, to straighten their lines. Konev's advance

took him to the line of the Neisse river, so that by the end of the month the two fronts were lined up only 40 miles (65km) from Berlin along 100 miles (160km) of the Oder and Neisse rivers. By the end of March, the 1st Belorussian Front had reached the sea at Kolberg and was opposite the great port of Stettin on the left bank of the Oder. In the south, meanwhile, the 1st and 4th Ukrainian Fronts had again pushed well forward into Czechoslovakia, defended by Field-Marshal Ferdinand Schörner's Army Group Center. Further south still, in Hungary, Budapest had fallen to Marshal R.Y. Malinovsky's 2nd Ukrainian Front on February 14, and the 2nd and 3rd Ukrainian Fronts had then pushed on to the general line, Nagyatad/Lake Balaton/Lake Velencei/Esztergom/ Banska Stiavnica by March 6. From here it was an easy push into the rest of Hungary and thence into Austria in the direction of Vienna.

But Hitler's desperate preoccupation with oil once again came into play: Colonel-General "Sepp" Dietrich's 6th SS Panzerarmee, resting in the area after its mauling in the Battle of the Bulge, was to strike south-east

between Lakes Balaton and Velencei to retake the Balaton oilfields. Other formations were to join in to the south to expand the offensive and administer a sharp check to the Soviets' general drive. Dietrich's offensive was launched on March 6, and at first good progress was made; but the weather was very bad, the ground thick with mud, and the Soviet defence steadfast. As the German armour was gradually slowed by the terrain and lack of fuel, the Soviets counterattacked, driving the Germans back. General Otto Wöhler's Army Group South could find no reply, and soon the 2nd and 3rd Ukrainian Fronts

ABOVE: U.S. troops, with a quadruple 0.5-inch (12.7-mm) machine-gun mounting, cover the approach to the Remagen bridge over the Rhine.

OPPOSITE ABOVE: A British mechanized column moves deeper into Germany as the defending forces begin to crumble.

OPPOSITE BELOW: Soviet "tank-rider" infantry move forward on a T-34/85 medium tank.

were over the border into Austria. Vienna fell on April 14, and a day later the Soviets were well beyond the city.

Between December 1944 and April 1945, therefore, the several Soviet fronts had pressed on from the line Kaunas/Bialystok/Warsaw/eastern Czechoslovakia/Budapest/Belgrade to a line from Stettin in the north to Vienna in the south, with a large German salient in eastern Czechoslovakia. Only in two places could the Germans make a defense in what was left of Germany, between the Western army groups advancing from France and the Soviets advancing from Poland and Czechoslovakia. By previous agreement at the Yalta Conference of February 1945, the western Allies were to halt on the Elbe river, west of Berlin, leaving the rest of Germany to the Soviets, with Berlin as the chief prize.

Under the overall supervision of Zhukov, the plans for the Berlin campaign were carefully laid. While the 2nd Belorussian Front drove across northern Germany from the Oder to the Elbe, the 1st Belorussian and 1st Ukrainian Fronts would close in on Berlin from the north and south, cut it off, and then fight their way in to final victory. Zhukov and Konev had no illusions about how bloody this fight would be. The figures of men and matériel are available for this climactic battle of the war against Germany. In Berlin itself, for example, were 2 million civilians and a garrison of 30,000. But holding the outer defenses were about 1 million German troops. To take on this formidable array, Zhukov and Konev could between them muster some 2.5 million men. Although the German troops were on the whole mediocre, with little in the way of munitions, the Soviets knew they would put up an excellent defence. The defenses themselves were mainly to the south of the city, for here there was no natural defense line such as the Havel river to the north. Of course, these were last-ditch defenses, and nothing like as strong as the German positions 40 miles (65km) away on the west bank of the Oder and Neisse rivers, which was the only place where there was a possible chance of beating the Soviets back.

The Soviet offensive started on April 16, preceded by one of the most intense artillery bombardments ever seen: along Zhukov and Konev's fronts there was one gun every 13 feet (4m). After enormously thorough artillery preparation the Soviets stormed across the rivers, only to be met by heavy fire. By April 18 the two Soviet fronts had each secured only two small bridgeheads, some 3 to 7 miles (5 to 11km) deep. Two days later, however, the Germans were crushed in scenes of terrible carnage. Zhukov and Konev pressed on as quickly as they could, and

linked up west of Berlin on April 25. The only part of the German river defense force to remain reasonably intact was the 9th Army, soon joined by part of the 4th Panzerarmee, in a pocket near Markisch Buchholz, some 30 miles (50km) south-east of Berlin.

The 2nd Belorussian Front attacked on April 20 and soon drove through the defenses of Colonel-General Kurt Student's Army Group Vistula. Army Group Center, well to the south of Berlin, had been split from the rest of the German defenses by Konev's wedge-shaped advance. On April 25 U.S. and Soviet forces met at Torgau on the Elbe, where the shattered remnants of the river defense forces were desperately trying to break through to the west before the Soviets' rear areas were consolidated.

Finally, it was Berlin against the 1st Belorussian and 1st Ukrainian Fronts as the Soviet attack was launched on April 26. By April 28 Zhukov's 2nd Guards Tank Army had reached the Spree river in the northern outskirts, but further to the south Konev's 8th Guards and 1st Guards Tank Armies had nearly reached the Tiergarten in the center of the city. If the two Soviet forces could only link up, Berlin would be cut into western and eastern halves. Hitler, by now totally demented, spent all of the time he had left calling on the 9th Army to break through and relieve the capital, which could by now barely hold its own. Although the two Soviet fronts were only 1 mile (1.5km) apart on April 28, it was to take them another four days of murderous close fighting to link up across the Reichstag and Chancellery, where Hitler's bunker was situated. On April 30, however, Hitler committed suicide, after appointing Grand-Admiral Karl Dönitz as his successor.

The fall of Berlin, in what was one of the bloodiest battles fought in the 20th century, left only one other major pocket of German resistance, namely Schörner's last-ditch defenses in Czechoslovakia. A diehard Nazi, Schörner had been given this command by Hitler because of his political loyalty. Although the war was lost, Schörner was determined to fulfil his orders to hold this important industrial area to the north-east of Prague, his methods of securing the cooperation of his men being that anyone refusing an order or showing any signs of sloth was shot. To the north was the 1st Ukrainian Front, to the east the 4th Ukrainian Front, to the south-east and south the 2nd Ukrainian Front, to the south-west the U.S. 3rd Army, and to the west the U.S. 1st Army. Only to the south was there any hope of escape, and here the 3rd Army and 3rd Ukrainian Front were hourly closing the gap. Schörner had some 1 million men, but without fuel and ammunition they were unable to halt the Allies. By April 6 the 2nd and 4th Ukrainian Fronts had overrun Slovakia in the east. A month later and they were well into the prosperous region of Moravia, but at this moment the Czech partisans arose in the Germans' rear, severely affecting their communications. Two days later, on May 8, the Soviets to the north, east and south launched a massive onslaught, in which Prague was taken on May 9. Schörner finally surrendered with his last German forces still fighting on May 11.

The Soviets estimated that German losses in the last three months of the war on the Eastern Front were 1 million civilians dead as well as 800,000 fighting men, with 12,000 armored vehicles, 23,000 guns and 6,000 aircraft captured.

While the Soviets were overcoming German resistance in the east, the western Allies were advancing. After the fighting in the Ardennes had died down, it would have been clear to anyone except Hitler that the only hope for Germany was an end to the war. This was not to be, and as long as the German army held together and could use the remnants of the Westwall, the floods in the Low Countries, and the barrier of the Rhine as a defensive system, it was plain that the task of defeating it would be long and bitter. It was for this reason that General Eisenhower insisted on the maximum concentration of force in France. The British were once more pressing for a main effort in the north, with Lieutenant General Patton clamouring for more action with as many divisions as possible in the 3rd Army sector, while General Jean de Lattre de Tassigny was demanding a greater share of the action for his French 1st army and for France. Eisenhower only considered these demands insofar as they suited the overall scheme, which was to uncover the Rhine from end to end by driving in the German bastions remaining on the west side. Then he intended to follow the classical strategy for forcing a river line by attacking on as many points as possible, "bouncing" a crossing where he could and making a formal assault with maximum artillery and air support where the defenses were strong, then advancing from these bridgeheads into the heart of Germany. The next move was to encircle the Ruhr industrial area on which the German economy depended, even though already wrecked by the bomber offensive, and mop it up, while the Allied armies drove forward to the Elbe to meet the Soviet forces.

The first move was by Lieutenant-General Jacob L. Devers's 6th Army Group in the south. A local counteroffensive, aimed at the recapture of Strasbourg, was beaten off in January and then the French 1st Army, its colonial troops much reduced in numbers after sacrificial fighting and suffering from cold and frostbite, were initially checked in an attempt to liquidate the "Colmar pocket," which was badly dented but still holding. Devers then reinforced the French with the U.S. XXI Corps and the attack was resumed. De Lattre deployed Major-General Leclerc's 2nd Armored Division, the Free French and his U.S. corps on the north of the salient, covering the nose which protruded into the Vosges with the French 10th Division, while his I Corps (2nd and 4th Moroccan Divisions and 9th Colonial Division) attacked from the south. The U.S. 109th Infantry Regiment drove the Germans from Colmar on February 1, chivalrously allowing the French troops to enter the city first. By February 5 the attacks from north and south had met, and by February 9 the

last Germans not already killed or captured were over the Rhine.

On February 8, away in the north, Field-Marshal Montgomery launched

the Canadian 1st Army, under General Sir Henry Crerar, into Operation Veritable, whose aim was to advance from the Nijmegen salient, break through

OPPOSITE: With a Soviet tank in the foreground, this is the end for Germany as Soviet warplanes fly over the ruined Reichstag.

ABOVE: Dead Waffen-SS men lie alongside their destroyed armoured personnel carrier.

RIGHT: One of Berlin's landmarks to remain only slightly damaged was the Brandenburg Gate.

65

the Westwall, clearing the Germans out of the Reichswald forest, Cleve, Goch, and Xanten. The attacks were planned with extreme care, with great reliance placed on powerful and highly skilled artillery. A fire plan of great complexity was prepared, first to suppress the German artillery and then to soften up the German positions, with special attention given to precise fire on concrete bunkers. Once the attack had started a barrage was to be put down on the forward enemy localities, to stand there for 70 minutes until the assaulting divisions closed up to the German positions; it would then begin to roll forward at the rate of 300 yards (275m) every 12 minutes, with six regiments on each divisional front providing four belts of fire altogether 500 yards (455m) deep. The total number of guns and howitzers employed was 1,050, supplemented by light antiaircraft guns, antitank guns, machine guns, the guns of tanks, heavy mortars, and a regiment of rocket-launchers. The Reichswald was cleared by February 13, Goch by February 21 and Xanten on February 26. This was the most severe fighting seen on the left bank of the Rhine, the 21st Army Group's casualties numbering 16,000

and the Germans losing 23,000 prisoners and an unknown number of killed and wounded.

On February 23 Lieutenant-General William H. Simpson's U.S. 9th Army, under command of the 21st Army Group, crossed the flooded valley of the Roer in assault boats (Operation Grenade), making sufficient progress to deploy armor by March 1. Simpson cleaned up his objectives with a loss of 7,300 men, but captured another 30,000 prisoners. These two battles went a long way to crack the still unbroken will of the German army.

In the meantime, the U.S. 1st Army of Lieutenant-General Courtney H. Hodges was grinding its way forward in the sector from Köln to Koblenz when the battles of attrition were enlivened by a flashing *coup de main* undertaking. The defenders were withdrawing in some confusion, and without a continuous front, when some U.S. tanks and armored infantry drove between them to capture Remagen, where they discovered that the Ludendorff Bridge across the Rhine was unblown and only lightly guarded as it was being used to allow the units still west of the Rhine to cross. This was reported and the local commander,

Brigadier-General William M. Hoge, ordered it to be seized. There was a blunder on the German side; the demolition charges were ready laid but when they were triggered only one exploded, causing a crater at the western end. The Americans rushed the bridge on foot under small arms fire, cutting the wires to the explosive charges as they went. Soon they had fought their way across, digging in on the far side. Curiously enough, Hoge's initiative was not followed up, the officers in the command chain referring ever upward until Lieutenant General Omar N. Bradley, at 12th Army Group headquarters, was reached. Bradley ordered Hodges to push across every formation he had in hand and by March 12 a bridgehead 14 miles (23km) wide was securely held by three divisions supported by tanks. In this way, the formidable obstacle was cheaply crossed and the way to the heart of Germany lay open. Counterattacks were beaten off, as were suicidal Luftwaffe missions, for a time, by a huge concentration of anti-aircraft artillery. But between the air attacks and a continual bombardment by heavy artillery the bridge collapsed. This was too late, for by that time the U.S. engineers had thrown sufficient bridges across the river to ensure that the forward troops could be maintained.

Lieutenant-General Patton, of the U.S. 3rd Army, was not to be outdone. He had a stiff task which needed to be undertaken methodically by stages, which did not suit his temperament, but which he nevertheless carried out with precision. He first broke through the

LEFT: One of the last photographs of Adolf Hitler, taken during an inspection of boy soldiers, before he committed suicide on 30 April 30, 1945.

OPPOSITE: At Reims, on May 7, 1945, Colonel-General Alfred Jodl, the chief of staff of the Oberkommando der Wehrmacht (armed forces high command), signs Germany's document of unconditional surrender on behalf of Grand-Admiral Karl Dönitz, Hitler's successor as head of state. On Jodl's left is General-Admiral Hans-Georg von Friedeburg, commander-in-chief of the German navy.

Westwall in the Saar and then crossed the Mosel, which meant an advance through broken and hilly country until he could uncover the Rhine from Koblenz to Mainz. He had his eyes fixed on the river, for he was determined to cross before Montgomery's projected date, March 24, and the day before managed to put six battalions across at Oppenheim at the cost of 28 casualties.

On March 31, anxious lest the Americans should cross the Rhine first, Jean de Lattre de Tassigny secured a bridgehead at Speyer.

On March 24 Montgomery launched his grand spectacular: Operations Plunder, the Rhine crossing, followed by Varsity, the airborne descent on the far side. This has been represented as an example of over-caution, but the same considerations also applied to Veritable. The German high command, which

was apprehensive about the northern thrust, had also made a fair appreciation of its scope and direction and one of the last of its good formations, the 1st Parachute Army, barred Montgomery's way. The river at his intended crossing point, between Emmerich and Homberg, is 1,000 yards (915m) wide and fast-flowing, and it was Montgomery's intention not to have a fight for the bridgehead but to drive through to a great depth in order that the subsequent advance could continue without check.

The planning for Plunder was based on the technique for landing on a coast rather than on a simple river crossing and, like Dragoon, embodied every possible refinement to ensure the crossing was successful and that there were minimal casualties. The main assault was to be carried out by the British 1st Commando Brigade, directed on Wesel,

the British 15th Division in the center of the British sector, and the U.S. 30th and 79th Divisions of Simpson's 9th Army south of the Lippe canal. H-hour was 2:00am on March 24. At 10:00am two airborne formations, the British 6th and the U.S. 17th Airborne Divisions, were to parachute in or be landed close enough to the river to be within supporting range of the artillery on the left bank.

In the British sector the difficulty of putting enough artillery across in the early stages made it necessary to deploy it in full view of the Germans on the right bank, and therefore a permanent smokescreen was generated to cover the whole front, while to aid maneuvers at night banks of searchlights, sited near the river, provided "artificial moonlight." The artillery fire plan was once more large and elaborate. Some 200 heavy bombers blasted a path for the

LEFT: *Field-Marshal Sir Bernard Montgomery presides over the surrender, by General-Admiral Hans-Georg von Friedeburg and General Hans Kinzel, of all the German forces in northern Germany, at Lüneberg Heath, south of Hamburg, on May 4, 1945.*

BELOW: *The room in which Adolf Hitler committed suicide on April 30, 1945.*

commandos as they approached Wesel, with more than 660 tanks poised to follow. Some of the Scots companies were in tracked amphibians (LVTs or Buffaloes) with orders not to disembark on the farther bank but to motor on, providing their own covering fire for objectives deep in the proposed bridgehead. The Scottish troops met with very strong resistance near the east bank, but were eventually able to clean it up.

By daylight, Eisenhower went to view the fly-in of 400 aircraft, carrying paratroops, followed by 1,300 more towing gliders, a total of 14,000 troops of the British 6th and U.S. 17th Airborne Divisions arriving in an endless procession which filled the sky. This required the most careful coordination with the field artillery fire, as shell trajectories were high enough to intersect the aircraft flight paths and meant that, at times, fire on the German antiaircraft artillery and other fire-support had to be denied. All went well, however, and by the end of the first day's fighting the British and Americans had joined up and were 6 miles (10km) beyond the river.

To the south Eisenhower's other two army groups were advancing from their bridgeheads, with no substantial resistance. It was estimated that only some 6,000 disorganized troops were opposing Devers. The orders for the December and January counteroffensives, followed by Hitler's desperate command to hold ground without yielding, had in fact left the surviving German formations in position for destruction. Some divisions were by now just headquarters and a few scratch troops, like the Volkssturm, and some were only combat teams (Kampfgruppen). Facing west, there was altogether only the equivalent of some 26 full-strength divisions, representing the last scrapings of German manpower. Nevertheless there would be much sharp fighting ahead, first on all fronts and then in pockets, as small groups of SS troops or paratroops decided to hold out to the bitter end.

The scheme of maneuver for the Ruhr battle was for the 9th Army to encircle the Ruhr from the north and the 1st Army from the south, linking at Lippstadt and trapping the German forces, who had intended using its cities to fight a long, delaying battle. This was complete by April 6. Three corps were given the task of entering the sack so formed, carving it up and reducing it sector by sector. Within was the headquarters of Army Group B, under Field-Marshal Walther Model, who refused a futile order from OKW to break out, but at the same time felt

unable to surrender formally. He told his troops to fight on or just go home as they chose, then committed suicide. Some 317,000 prisoners, including two dozen generals, representing some 19 divisions and various army and corps headquarters, plus 100,000 air defense troops, were captured.

While this last great battle of the war in the west was going on, the remaining U.S. armies were surging forward to the Elbe with ever-increasing momentum, while farther north the Canadians and British advanced against more dogged resistance from formed bodies of troops. Eisenhower then made a major alteration to his final plan. He had originally intended to make Berlin his final objective, but a number of considerations supervened. Allied intelligence believed the Germans might take to guerrilla warfare and that there was a plan to establish a "national redoubt" in the mountains of Bavaria, so he ordered the U.S. 3rd and 7th Armies to swing south. To go on to Berlin, Eisenhower estimated, might be too costly to be worthwhile so late in the war. With the main German armies facing him destroyed, Berlin had ceased to be a purely military objective, apart from which the Soviets were closer to it than he was himself. He feared that a head-on contact between the Soviets and

Allied troops might lead to awkward confrontations, and sought some clear natural feature on which they could meet in orderly fashion, for which he regarded the Elbe as ideal. He also felt that there was little point in capturing territory only to hand it back to the Soviets according to political agreements already entered into by the Allies. He therefore resisted the British demands to be allowed to go on to Berlin and also Simpson's similar request when he had secured a bridgehead over the Elbe. On April 24 officers of the U.S. V Corps met Soviet representatives at Torgau on the Elbe and the forward movement ceased.

With Hitler's death on April 30, what central authority there was disappeared, and the Reich began to surrender piecemeal. The representatives of the Germans in the north surrendered to Montgomery, with effect from 8:00am on May 5. At the same time, large German forces, east of the Elbe, surrendered to Simpson, many civilians attempting to cross to the west bank to escape the Soviets. For a formal surrender the Allies insisted on complete capitulation on both fronts, and this took place at the Allied supreme headquarters in Reims in France at 2.00am on May 7.

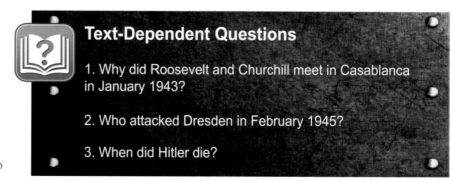

Text-Dependent Questions

1. Why did Roosevelt and Churchill meet in Casablanca in January 1943?

2. Who attacked Dresden in February 1945?

3. When did Hitler die?

Research Projects

Summarize all the main events in April and May 1945 leading up to the end of World War II in Europe.

Chapter Eight
THE ITALIAN CAMPAIGN COMES TO AN END

During the spring of 1945 the same opponents faced each other in Italy: the Allied 5th and 8th Armies, and the German 10th and 14th Armies. Only some of the principal actors had changed roles. Field-Marshals Albert Kesselring and Sir Harold Alexander had become theater commanders, the latter of all the Allied forces in the Mediterranean. Army Group C was now led by the excellent Colonel-General Heinrich von Vietinghoff, and the ambitious Lieutenant-General Mark W. Clark had succeeded Alexander in command of the 15th Army Group. Major-General Lucian K. Truscott, who had commanded the US VI Corps at Anzio, in succession to Lieutenant-General John P. Lucas, now led the U.S. 5th Army, and Lieutenant-General Sir Oliver Leese, transferred to Burma, was succeeded by Lieutenant-General Sir Richard McCreery.

Alexander's orders from the Combined Chiefs of Staff Committee for 1945 had been to continue with the pressure on Army Group C, hard enough to prevent the withdrawal of any German divisions from Italy, and if von Vietinghoff withdrew to a new defense line in the foothills of the Alps, to follow him. This was an invitation to limit operations to a few cautious, small-scale attacks. Two more good divisions of Canadians had been taken away to strengthen the Canadian army on the Western Front, and although Clark had received a Brazilian division and a specialist U.S. mountain division fresh from the USA, and McCreery two Polish brigades and a Jewish Palestinian brigade, the numerical odds against the 15th Army Group were still 17 to 23 against in terms of divisions.

The war was nearly over. Eisenhower's armies had crossed the Rhine in three places in March, the Soviet vanguards were at the frontier of Austria, Army Group C was well equipped and up to strength and in an extremely strong position, and there was no point in incurring many more casualties. Moreover, a German emissary was secretly in touch with Alexander's headquarters concerning the possibility of a negotiated surrender in Italy. Another costly offensive, it could be argued, that made little sense. Alexander and his commanders were of a different opinion. Their deficiency in manpower was more than offset by their superiority in armor, artillery, and air power, so they continued to argue that the only way to carry out their mission effectively was to mount a full-scale offensive. They felt they had fought too hard and for too long to relax now without the victory they believed to be rightly theirs and, strangely enough, so also did the soldiers.

The Italian front was divided by geography into two distinct sectors, both ideally suited for defense. Opposite the U.S. 5th Army the road north was barred by 10 miles (16km) of crags and precipices, fortified and garrisoned by the best of the German infantry. The British 8th Army's front line was along the flood banks of the Senio river, and four more defended river lines lay beyond. On the right the way was barred by the waters of Lake Comacchio and floods created by the breaching of the dykes along the rivers. Across the whole 50 miles (80km) of front there was only one dry gap, where the road north to Argenta ran between the lake and the floods, offering a way round the whole river network. McCreery fixed his sights on this.

Clark's plan was for the 8th Army to attack early in April, using all the air power available, and that when McCreery had attracted the German reserves to the east, the 5th Army would in its turn take it over for a thrust in the center. The 8th Army's last offensive was a triumphant combination of tactics and technology. A large number of DD amphibious tanks and tracked amphibious infantry carriers had reached the theater, and these converted the expanse of water facing the 8th Army's right from a barrier to an avenue reaching the heart of the 10th

Army's defenses. As a first move British commandos and Royal Marines secured a safe start line on the south and east of Lake Comacchio, and then two brigades of the 56th Division in assault boats attacked the eastern shore and secured the wedge of dry land leading to Argenta. This was the doorway through which McCreery intended to pass his armour. If the bridge over the Reno river at Bastia could be secured he would have the side door to the whole of the 10th Army's defense system, for then, after crossing the Senio, his right-hand divisions could link with the 56th Division and fan out toward the Po.

On April 9 the 10th Army's artillery areas received thousands of tons of fragmentation bombs from heavy bombers, then by medium bombers, followed by fighter-bombers in close support of the attacking infantry. A series of barrages were fired from 1,000 guns. The far bank was doused with burning fuel from flame-throwing tanks, and the assault began. The infantry crossed, followed by tanks and the welter of specialist armored vehicles. By April 16 the 10th Army was still fighting doggedly, but the veteran 6th Armoured, 78th and 56th Divisions had fanned out north of Argenta in the Po valley and were inching forward. Von Vietinghoff's line was near breaking point.

Truscott began his attack in clear skies on April 14. It was a sign of the times, perhaps, when a German division in defence actually disintegrated and ran. The U.S. 10th Mountain Division was enthusiastic and fresh, and it had been specifically trained in mountain warfare, unlike the normal U.S. troops. Now, in the same manner as the Moroccan *goumiers* in the Gustav Line, the

American mountain troops led the way through the remaining northern foothills of the Apennines. The remnants of the 14th Army had to come down from the peaks or be cut off. Truscott's main thrust was directed east of Bologna, because one of the peculiarities of von Vietinghoff's position was that its final stop-line was the Reno river, which curled all around his center and left, but could be outflanked in the west by Truscott where it rose in the Apennines, or at the Argenta gap. The Americans and British were now moving with great impetus, while throughout the back areas of Army Group C the RAF and the USAAF were ready to pounce on any movement of German troops.

It was Clark's desire to catch the whole German force south of the Po, and to destroy it there with the river at its back: this he achieved. Any remote possibility that it could have escaped had been denied by Hitler himself. Before the Allied offensive had started von Vietinghoff had asked for Hitler's permission to fight a mobile battle of withdrawal and so keep his army intact, but was accused of "wavering" and of revealing "defeatist attitudes," and

ordered to hold. When von Vietinghoff finally ordered a withdrawal his front had already collapsed. As he had foreseen, the only hope would have been to have ducked the hammer blows of Allied air power and artillery and to have slipped back across the wide and flooded Po.

On April 22 the South African 6th Division, leading the 5th Army's advance, and the British 6th Armoured Division traveling west, met each other behind the retreating Germans at a village appropriately called Finale. The Germans were trapped and in complete disorder, except on the Mediterranean coast, where a mountain corps remained in good order until the end. Even the paratroops began to surrender. Most of the German heavy equipment was left on the south bank, the units which had got away having been harried by the Italian partisans, while the Allied divisions, hardly able to realize that their battle was won, crossed the Po and raced for the Alpine passes. The cease-fire was ordered for 6:00pm hours on May 2. It had been 21 months and 13 days since the touchdown on the Sicilian beaches, and the long, bitter and forgotten war was finally over.

OPPOSITE: *Two troopers of the Special Air Service and an Italian partisan near Castino, in northern Italy, during April 1945. SAS operations behind the German lines made German communications almost impossible.*

RIGHT: *Italian partisans and civilians at the time of the German surrender.*

WORLD WAR II
TIME LINE OF WORLD WAR II

1939
Germany invades Poland on September 1.

Two days later Britain and France declare war on Germany.

1940
Rationing starts in the UK.

German "Blitzkrieg" overwhelms and overpowers Belgium, Holland, and France.

Churchill becomes Prime Minister of Britain.

British Expeditionary Force evacuated from Dunkirk.

Britain is victorious in the Battle of Britain. Hitler to postpones invasion plans.

1941
Operation Barbarossa commences – the invasion of Russia begins.

The Blitz continues against Britain. Major cities are badly damaged.

Allies take Tobruk in North Africa, and resist German attacks.

Japan attacks Pearl Harbor, and the U.S. enters the war.

1942
Germany suffers setbacks at Stalingrad and El Alamein.

Singapore falls to the Japanese in February – around 25,000 prisoners taken.

American naval victory at Battle of Midway, in June, marks turning point in Pacific War.

Mass murder of Jewish people at Auschwitz begins.

1943
Germany surrenders at Stalingrad. Germany's first major defeat.

The Allies are victorious in North Africa The invasion of Italy is launched.

Italy surrenders to the Allies, but Germany takes over the fight.

British and Indian forces fight Japanese in Burma.

1944
Allies land at Anzio and bomb monastery at Monte Cassino.

Soviet offensive gathers pace in Eastern Europe.

D-Day: The Allied invasion of France. Paris is liberated in August.

Guam liberated by the U.S. *Okinawa*, and Iwo Jima bombed.

1945
Auschwitz liberated by Soviet troops. Russians reach Berlin. Hitler commits suicide and Germany surrenders on May 7.

Truman becomes President of the U.S. on Roosevelt's death.

Attlee replaces Churchill.

After atomic bombs are dropped on Hiroshima and Nagasaki, Japan surrenders on August 14.

OPPOSITE: *Operation Market Garden. Nijmegen. After the battle. September 28,1944.*

Series Glossary of Key Terms

Allied Powers A coalition of nations that fought against the Axis powers.

ANZAC An Australian or New Zealand soldier.

Appeasement A policy of agreeing to hostile demands in order to maintain peace.

Aryan In Nazi ideology, a Caucasian especially of Nordic type.

Auschwitz An industrial town in Poland and site of Nazi concentration camp during World War II.

Axis Powers An alignment of nations that fought against the Allied forces in World War II.

Blitzkrieg A surprise and violent offensive by air and ground forces.

Concentration camp A camp where prisoners of war are detained or confined.

D-Day June 6, 1944. The Allied invasion of France in World War II began.

Fascism A political movement or philosophy that exalts nation and race above the individual with an autocratic government and a dictator as leader.

Führer A leader or tyrant.

Final Solution The Nazi program to exterminate all the Jews throughout Europe.

Gestapo A secret-police employing devious ways of controlling people considered disloyal.

Holocaust The mass slaughter of European civilians especially the Jews by the Nazis during World War II.

Kamikaze A Japanese pilot trained to make suicidal crash attacks upon ships in World War II.

Lebensraum Territory considered necessary by Nazis for national existence.

Luftwaffe German air force.

Maginot Line Defensive fortifications on the eastern border of France during World War II.

Manhattan Project The code name for the secret U.S. project set up in 1942 to develop an atomic bomb.

Nazi An advocate of policies characteristic of Nazism.

Pact of Steel A military alliance between Nazi Germany and Fascist Italy concluded on May 22, 1939.

Panzer A German tank.

Potsdam Conference A conference held in Potsdam in the summer of 1945 where Roosevelt, Stalin, and Churchill drew up plans for the adminstration of Germany and Poland after World War II ended.

U-boat A German submarine especially in World War I and II.

The Versailles Treaty The treaty imposed on Germany by the Alllied powers in 1920 after the end of World War I.

Yalta Conference A conference held in Yalta in February 1945, where Roosevelt, Stalin, and Churchill planned the finals statge of World War II and agreed to new boundaries and territorial division in Europe.

Further Reading and Internet Resources

WEBSITES

http://www.bbc.co.uk/history/worldwars/wwtwo

http://www.history.com/topics/world-war-ii

https://www.britannica.com/event/World-War-II

http://www.world-war-2.info/

BOOKS

Hourly History. *World War II The Definitive Visual Guide.* Oxford University Press, 2010

Richard Overy. *The New York Times Complete World War II: The Coverage of the Entire Conflict.* 2016

Smithsonian. *World War II The Definitive Visual Guide* DK Publishing Inc., 2015.

If you enjoyed this book take a look at Mason Crest's other war series:

The Civil War, The Vietnam War, Major U.S. Historical Wars.

In this book, page numbers in ***bold italic font*** indicate photos or videos.

A

air force
    Battle of Arnhem, *6,* 48–54, *49–50, 52–53, 73*
    Battle of the Bulge, *2,* 55, *55,* 57
    Battle of Kursk, 14, 16
    bomber offensive, 21, 38, 40–41, 58–61, *59–61, 73*
    British, 18, 30, 32–33, 36–41, *40 ,* 43, *45,* 48–52, *49–50, 53 ,* 58–61, *59–61,* 67, 69, *70,* 71
    end of war role, 61–62, *64,* 66, 67, 69, *70,* 70–71
    France invasion, *35,* 36–41, *40, 42,* 43, *45*
    German, *2, 5,* 14, 16, 18, *30,* 33, 50, 55, 58–61, 62, 66, 67, 71
    gliderborne troops, 18–19, *35,* 38, *42,* 51, *52,* 69
    Italian, 18
    Italy invasion/battles, 18–19, 21, 30, *30,* 32–33, *70,* 70–71
    Operation Dragoon, *42,* 43
    Operation Overlord, *35,* 36–41, *40*
    parachute divisions, *2, 6,* 18–19, *30,* 33, 38, *40, 42,* 43, 48–54, *49–50, 52–53,* 55, *55,* 67, 69, *70,* 71
    Polish, 53
    Romanian, 58
    Soviet, 16, 24, 27, 61–62, *64*
    Soviet-Axis battles, 14, 16, 24, 27, 61–62, *64*
    US, *6,* 18–19, 21, 32–33, 36–41, *40, 42,* 43, 49–52, *52,* 54, *55,* 57, 58–61, *59–61,* 67, 69, 70–71
Alexander, Harold, 18–19, 21, 22, 23, 30, 33–34, 70
Algerian soldiers, 22, 32, 43, 45
Allied Powers
    Battle of Arnhem, *6,* 48–54, *48–54, 73*
    Battle of the Bulge, *2,* 55–57, *55–57*
    Battle of Kursk, 12–17, *12–17*
    bomber offensive, 21, 38, 40–41, 58–61, *59–61, 73*
    end of war by, 61–71, *62–68, 70–71*

France invasion, *8,* 30, 32–33, 35–47, *35–47,* 59
Italy invasion/liberation, 17, 18–23, *18–23,* 30–35, *30–35,* 70–71, *70–71*
Operation Dragoon, 30, *42–44,* 42–45
Operation Overlord, *8,* 30, 32–33, 35–41, *35–41*
Soviet Union battles, *3,* 12–17, *12–17,* 24–29, *24–29,* 61–64, *63, 64*
See also specific countries
Anzio, Allied invasion at, 21–22, 23, 32
armistices, *22,* 29
See also Germany: surrender of
Atlantic Wall, 35, *35*
Austria, Soviet-Axis battles in, 62, 63
Axis Forces
    Battle of Arnhem, *6,* 48–54, *48–54, 73*
    Battle of the Bulge, *2,* 55–57, *55–57*
    Battle of Kursk, 12–17, *12–17*
    bomber offensive against, 21, 38, 40–41, 58–61, *59–61, 73*
    end of war for, 61–71, *62–68, 70–71*
    France invasion response, 30, 32–33, 35–47, *35–47,* 59
    Italy invasion/battles response, 17, 18–23, *18–23,* 30–35, *30–35,* 70–71, *70–71*
    Operation Dragoon against, 30, *42–44,* 42–45
    Operation Overlord against, *8,* 30, 32–33, 35–41, *35–41*
    Soviet Union battles/expulsion, *3,* 12–17, *12–17,* 24–29, *24–29,* 61–64, *63, 64*
    See also specific countries

B

Bagramyan, I. K., 27, 61
Battle of Arnhem, *6,* 48–54, *48–54, 73*
Battle of the Beach-head, 36, 41
Battle of Berlin, 59
Battle of the Bulge, *2,* 55–57, *55–57*
Battle of Kursk, 12–17, *12–17*
Battle of Normandy, 36, 46
Belgium, Battle of the Bulge in, *2,* 55–57, *55–57*
Berlin, end of war in, 63–64, *65,* 69
Bittrich, Willi, 50–51, 53

bomber offensive, 21, 38, 40–41, 58–61, *59–61, 73*
Bor-Komorowski, Tadeusz, 28
Bradley, Omar N., 38–39, 40–41, 42, 47, 55, 57, 66
Brandenburger, Erich, 55
Brazil, end of war role of, 70
Brereton, Lewis H., 48
Brosset, Charles Joseph, 43–44
Bulgaria, Soviet-Axis battles and surrender of, 29, 61
Busch, Ernst, 27–28

C

Canada
    Battle of Arnham role of, *51*
    end of war role of, 65, 69, 70
    France invasion role of, 35, 38, 39, 40, 41, 46, *47*
    Italy invasion role of, 21, 31–32, 33, 34
Cassino/Monte Cassino, 21–23, 32–33, *34*
casualties
    British, 34–35, 52, 54, 66
    German, 16, 26, 27–28, 44, 54, 55, 59, 64, *65,* 66
    New Zealand, 23
    Polish, 33
    Soviet, 24, 25, 26
    US, 52, 57, 58, 59
Chernyakovsky, I. D., 27, 61
Churchill, Winston, 30, 58
Clark, Mark W., 20, 33, 70–71
Crerar, Henry, 65
Czechoslovakia, Soviet-Axis battles in, 61, 62, 63, 64

D

D-Day, 37–39, *38–39*
    See also Operation Overlord
de Lattre de Tassigny, Jean Marie Gabriel, 42–44, 64–65, 67
Devers, Jacob L., 42, 43, 65, 69
Diadem, 23, 30, 32
Dietrich, "Sepp," 55, 62
Dönitz, Karl, 64, *67*
Dresden, bombing of, *60,* 61

PHOTOGRAPHIC ACKNOWLEDGEMENTS

All images in this book are supplied by Cody Images and are in the public domain.

The contents of this book was first published as *WORLD WAR II*.

ABOUT THE AUTHOR

Christopher Chant

Christopher Chant is a successful writer on aviation and modern military matters, and has a substantial number of authoritative titles to his credit. He was born in Cheshire, England in December 1945, and spent his childhood in East Africa, where his father was an officer in the Colonial Service. He returned to the UK for his education at the King's School, Canterbury (1959–64) and at Oriel College, Oxford (1964–68). Aviation in particular and military matters in general have long been a passion, and after taking his degree he moved to London as an assistant editor on the Purnell partworks, *History of the Second World War* (1968–69) and *History of the First World War* (1969–72). On completion of the latter he moved to Orbis Publishing as editor of the partwork, *World War II* (1972–74), on completion of which he decided to become a freelance writer and editor.

Living first in London, then in Lincolnshire after his marriage in 1978, and currently in Sutherland, at the north-western tip of Scotland, he has also contributed as editor and writer to the partworks, *The Illustrated Encyclopedia of Aircraft*, *War Machine*, *Warplane*, *Take-Off*, *World Aircraft Information Files* and *World Weapons*, and to the magazine *World Air Power Journal*. In more recent years he was also involved in the creation of a five-disk CR-ROM series, covering the majority of the world's military aircraft from World War I to the present, and also in the writing of scripts for a number of video cassette and TV programs, latterly for Continuo Creative.

As sole author, Chris has more than 90 books to his credit, many of them produced in multiple editions and co-editions, including more than 50 on aviation subjects. As co-author he has contributed to 15 books, ten of which are also connected with aviation. He has written the historical narrative and technical database for a five-disk *History of Warplanes* CD-ROM series, and has been responsible for numerous video cassette programs on military and aviation matters, writing scripts for several TV programmes and an A–Z 'All the World's Aircraft' section in Aerospace/Bright Star *World Aircraft Information Files* partwork. He has been contributing editor to a number of books on naval, military and aviation subjects as well as to numerous partworks concerned with military history and technology. He has also produced several continuity card sets on aircraft for publishers such as Agostini, Del Prado, Eaglemoss, Edito-Service and Osprey.